JANUARY 2022 EDITION

AN ANTHOLOGY OF ARTICLES

BRILLOPEDIA

Contents

Contents

Preface

"Start writing, no matter what. The water does not flow until the faucet is turned on".

-Louis L'Amour

This book is a bouquet of articles contributed by students, professors and academicians. Hundreds of students and professors are contributing their work to Brillopedia, we are here to provide ample information about Law and Contemporary issues. Our aim is to provide a platform for today's generation to express their views and ideas on law and contemporary law.

CHAPTER ONE

LAWS REGULATING DRUGS AND COSMETICS IN INDIA AND THE UNITED STATES OF AMERICA

Author: Vanathi Krishna K, IV year of B.B.A.,LL.B.(Hons.) from Sastra Deemed to be University, Thanjavur

ABSTRACT

Drugs and Cosmetics hold paramount importance in the lives of the earthborn. Drugs are substances that succour the body to be physically and psychologically well balanced. Cosmetics aid to ameliorate or alter the appearance of the countenance and the body which includes personal care, skin care, fragrance, etc. Since drugs and cosmetics serve most of the indispensable necessities of human life, it is inevitable to regulate them. In this research piece, the author has analysed and explored the laws regulating Drugs and Cosmetics in India and the United States of America. Drugs and Cosmetics are regulated by the Drugs and Cosmetics Act of 1940 in India and by the Federal Food, Drug and Cosmetic Act of 1938 in the USA. This paper commences with the legal definitions of drugs and cosmetics under both acts. Further, the regulations of drugs categorised under different schedules and labelling requirements are explored. This paper is shaped to throw light on various offences and penalties and relevant judgments having reference to drugs and cosmetics under the respective acts.

INTRODUCTION

The Drugs and Cosmetics Act of 1940 which regulates drugs and cosmetics in India consists of 5 chapters and 38 sections.[i]

Chapter I (Sections 1 to 4)	Title, application, definitions and certain presumptions
Chapter II (Sections 5 to 7A)	The Drugs Technical Advisory Board, The Central Drugs Laboratory and The Drugs Consultative Committee
Chapter III (Sections 8 to 15)	Import of drugs and cosmetics
Chapter IV (Sections 16 to 33A)	Manufacture, sale and distribution of drugs and cosmetics
Chapter IV- A (Sections 33B to 33O)	Provisions relating to Ayurveda, Siddha and Unani drugs
Chapter V (Sections 33P to 38)	Miscellaneous

The Federal Food, Drug and Cosmetic Act (FDCA) of 1938 which regulates drugs and Cosmetics in the U.S consists of 10 chapters.[i]

Chapter I	Short Title
Chapter II	Definitions
Chapter III	Prohibited Acts and Penalties
Chapter IV	Food
Chapter V	Drugs and devices
Chapter VI	Cosmetics
Chapter VII	General Authority
Chapter VIII	Imports and Exports
Chapter IX	Tobacco Products
Chapter X	Miscellaneous

---

[i] https://www.indiacode.nic.in/handle/123456789/2409?sam_handle=123456789/1362

DEFINITION OF DRUGS

Section 3(b) of the Drugs and Cosmetics Act, 1940 defines 'Drugs' as

- All medicines for internal or external use of human beings or animals and all substances intended to be used for or in the diagnosis, treatment, mitigation or prevention of any disease or disorder in human beings or animals, including preparations applied on the human body for the purpose of repelling insects like mosquitoes.
- Such substances (other than food) intended to affect the structure or any function of the human body or intended to be used for the destruction of vermin or insects which cause disease in human beings or animals, as may be specified from time to time by the Central Government by notification in the Official Gazette.
- All substances intended for use as components of a drug including empty gelatine capsules.
- Such devices intended for internal or external use in the diagnosis, treatment, mitigation or prevention of disease or disorder in human beings or animals, as may be specified from time to time by the Central Government by notification in the Official Gazette, after consultation with the Board.[ii]

Section 201(g)(1) of the Federal Food, Drugs and Cosmetics Act, 2004 expounds the meaning of drugs as follows:

- Articles recognised in the official United States pharmacopeia, official homeopathic pharmacopeia of the United States or official National Formulary, or any supplement to any of them.
- Articles intended for use in the diagnosis, cure, mitigation, treatment, or prevention of disease in man or other animals.
- Articles (other than food) intended to affect the structure or any function of the body of man or other animals.[iii]

Stating simply, drugs are substances or medicines that assist in diagnosing and treating both internal as well as external diseases and disorders of human beings and animals. It includes insect repellents, vaccines, antibiotics, antigens, antitoxins, antibiotics, antiseptic, etc.

DEFINITION OF COSMETICS

Section 201(i) of the Federal Food, Drugs and Cosmetics Act and Section 3(aaa) of the Drugs and Cosmetics Act elucidates Cosmetics as

"Articles intended to be rubbed, poured, sprinkled, or sprayed on, introduced into, or otherwise applied to the human body or any part thereof for cleansing, beautifying, promoting attractiveness, or altering the appearance."

The Federal Food, Drugs and Cosmetics Act of the USA excludes soaps from the category of Cosmetics. In consonance with the FD&C Act, a product may be deemed merely as a drug, merely as a cosmetic and also as both drug and cosmetic.

For instance,

An anti-dandruff shampoo meets the requirements of both drugs and cosmetics. It is a cosmetic as it cleanses the hair and also a drug since it contains anti-dandruff ingredients to treat dandruff.

LAWS REGULATING DRUGS AND COSMETICS IN INDIA

In India, the Drugs and Cosmetics Act, of 1940 has been enacted to regulate the import, manufacture, sales and distribution of drugs and cosmetics through a valid licence. Subsequently, the Drug Rules were passed in 1945. This act prescribes standards of quality and specific guidelines for the storage, labelling and display of drugs and cosmetics. The main objective of this act is to ensure that the drugs and cosmetics that are sold in India are in consonance with the state quality standards and to ensure that the manufacture, sales and distribution are carried out by qualified persons under this act. Ayurveda, Siddha and Unani drugs are also governed by this act. Furthermore, this act laid down penalties of imprisonment and fine for any offence contravening the provisions of this act. The initial amendment of this act was done in 2008. Recently, the 10th amendment of the Drugs and Cosmetic Rules, 2017 proclaimed that the licence for the manufacture and sale of drugs once issued shall remain perpetually provided that the licensee deposits the retention fee for the licence every five years.[iv]

Regulations of Drugs

As aforementioned, drugs are any substances that are purported to stabilize the physiological and psychological functions of the body. The Drugs and Cosmetics Act, 1940 expounds the terms 'Misbranded Drugs', 'Adulterated Drugs' and 'Spurious Drugs'.

Misbranded Drugs: Section 9 and 17 of the act elucidates Misbranded Drugs as drugs that are coloured, overlaid or laminated to conceal any damages or made it seem to be of possessing greater therapeutic value than the normal standard value of the drug.

Adulterated Drugs: Adulterated drugs are drugs that are incorporated with any decayed, petrified, toxic substances in addition to the essential ingredients which are detrimental to human and animal health as defined under Section 9A and 17A of this act.

Spurious Drugs: Spurious drugs are imitated drugs that lack their own identity and are almost fairly identical to another drug or imported under the name of another drug or manufactured under a name of a fictitious company.

The Drugs and Cosmetics Act categorizes the drugs under Schedules and furnishes guidelines for the storage, labelling and packaging for each schedule respectively. Here are some prime schedules.

Schedule C/C1-Biological drugs

Schedule G- Hormonal preparations

Schedule H- Drugs that are sold only under the prescription of a Registered Medical Practitioner.

Schedule J- Drugs that are not legally claimed to cure diseases such as AIDS, blindness, etc.

Schedule F/F- Blood Products/ Vaccines

Section 10 and 18 of this Act prohibits the import and manufacture & sale of certain drugs respectively which are incorporated by the Central Government by notification in the official gazette i.e. Drugs of non-standard quality, Misbranded, Adulterated, Spurious drugs, etc.,

Section 10A and 26A of this Act empowers the Central Government to prohibit the import and manufacture & sales of any drugs respectively in the public interest or on the ground if the drugs or any ingredient in the drugs do not have any therapeutic value.

Regulation of Cosmetics

Section 9C and 17C of the Drugs and Cosmetics Act, 1940 patently defines Misbranded Cosmetics and 9D and 17D of this act defines Spurious Cosmetics. Adulterated Cosmetics are elucidated under section 17E of this act.

For the manufacture, sale and distribution of cosmetics under this Act, the manufacturer should get hold of a license under Form 31 with a license and inspection fee of Rs. 2500/- and Rs.1000/- respectively. Besides, the manufacturer should possess a premise as prescribed under Schedule MII of this Act.

Prerequisites of Labelling

Name of the drug or cosmetic as prescribed, Net Quantity, Batch Number, Manufacturing License Number, Import License Number, Name and Address of the manufacturer, Manufactured and Expiry date are the labelling requirements of both drugs and cosmetics.

For the drugs of Schedule G -warning and caution; Schedule H- the symbols Rx or NRx with the warning "To be sold under the prescription of the Registered Medical Practitioner Only" should be labelled under this Act. For cosmetics, the direction of use, warning and caution should mandatorily be labelled in the inner and outer container.

Offences and Penalties

Any person who manufactures spurious drugs shall be punished with the imprisonment of 1-3 years with a fine of Rs.500/- and 2-6 years with Rs. 10,000/- on subsequent convictions.

For the manufacturing of Adulterated drugs, the punishment is imprisonment for 1 year with a fine of Rs. 2000/- and 2 years with Rs. 2000/- on subsequent convictions.

Any person who import Spurious drugs and cosmetics and Adulterated drugs and cosmetics that are in contravention to section 10A of this Act shall be punished with the imprisonment of 3 years or a fine of Rs.5000 or both on the first conviction and 5 years or Rs. 10,000/- or both on subsequent convictions.

M/s. Prem Pharmaceuticals and Others. V. State of Madhya Pradesh[v]

In this instant case, the petitioners were prosecuted under the Drugs and Cosmetics Act on the ground that their sodium chloride injection was of sub-standard quality and contained extraneous particles. The Indore Bench of Madhya Pradesh High Court quashed the prosecution and held that in the absence of a proper analysis of the particles in the medicine, it is irrelevant to say that the particles are of extraneous nature and not the ingredient of the medicine that came into existence during the manufacture and storage. Further, the court observed that according to section 19(2)(b) of the Drugs and Cosmetics Act, a drug shall not be deemed to be of sub-standard quality if some extraneous substance has been inexorably intermixed with it.

<u>**LAWS REGULATING DRUGS AND COSMETICS IN THE USA**</u>

The Federal Food, Drug and Cosmetic Act (1938) is a Federal law that was enacted to establish, oversee and enforce the quality standards of food, drugs, cosmetics and medical devices manufactured and sold in the United

States of America. The Pure Drug and Food Act, the first law enacted in 1906 for the federal regulation of food and pharmaceutical industries, was replaced by the Federal Food, Drug and Cosmetic Act of 1938 owing to the Elixir Sulfanilamide disaster. The FD&C Act has several times been amended since 1938. The main objective of amending the act was to ameliorate the efficacy of the established drugs since 1938. The Human Resources (HR) introduced the Safe Cosmetics Act of 2010 to expand the regulation of cosmetics.[vi]

Chapter V of the act deals with Drugs and Devices. Section 501 and 502 of the FD&C Actinterpret the terms 'Adulterated drugs and devices' and 'Misbranded drugs and devices' respectively. These definitions look much more natural in both the Drugs and Cosmetics Act of India and the FD&C Act of the USA. Chapter VI of the FD&C Act deals with Cosmetics. The FDA under FD&C Act does not approve cosmetics whereas it inspects and prohibits the manufacture and marketing of misbranded or adulterated cosmetics. In the USA, it is not imperative for any company to avail premarket approval or registration for the manufacture of cosmetics. However, they can submit the information of the products of their own volition through Voluntary Cosmetic Registration Program (VCRP) and Food & Drug Administration (FDA)to avoid any predicaments in future.

Prerequisites of labelling

Drugs - Name of the drug as prescribed, Name and the net quantity of each component, Name and Address of the manufacturer, packer and distributor, Lot number and Batch number should be labelled. Further, the manufactured and Expiry date should be labelled both on the inner container and outer package. For Over Counter (OTC) drugs (i.e.) the drugs that can be sold without a prescription from a medical practitioner, the warning about the usage of the drug during pregnancy or breastfeeding should be labelled.

Cosmetic - In the USA, cosmetic labelling is regulated by both the FD&C Act and FPLA (Fair Packaging and Labelling Act). An explicit declaration of the ingredients in the package is required for the products manufactured for retail sale as suggested by the Cosmetics, Toiletries and Fragrances Association (CTFA). For imported cosmetic products, the country of origin should be labelled.

Offences and Penalties

'Mens rea' or intention is not a predominant element under the FD&C Act. The three main elements for a criminal conviction under this act is

(i) Whether the article is a food or drug or medical device or cosmetic.

(ii) Whether the article is adulterated or misbranded.

(iii) Whether the article is introduced into interstate commerce.

Section 303(a) of this act establishes penalties for any criminal infringement of the act (misdemeanours) and for any criminal act with an intention to defraud or mislead (Felonies). For simple violations of the act, the accused shall be punished with imprisonment which may extend to 1 year or a fine of $1,000 or both. Any person who has a guilty mind to defraud or mislead shall be punished with imprisonment for up to 3 years or a fine up to $10,000 or both. The current maximum fine for an individual for misdemeanours not resulting in death is $100,000 and for misdemeanours resulting in death is $250,000. In the case of an organisation, the maximum fine for misdemeanours not resulting in death is $200,000 and misdemeanours resulting in death are $500,000.[vii]

The United States. V. Park[viii]

The defendant Park, CEO of Acme International had failed to comply with the conditions laid down by the Food, Drug and Cosmetic Act for warehouse sanitation. The Supreme Court of the United States held that Park was strictly liable for the unhygienic condition that his company had created. Further, the court held that the FD&C Act being a welfare statute, its chief purpose is to avert appalling harm in the society and also held that the Food and Drug Administration(FDA) under FD&C Act could penetrate the corporate veil.

<u>CONCLUSION</u>

Safety and efficacy are the two prime elements for the enactment of the laws regulating drugs and cosmetics. Drugs and cosmetics are regulated by various bodies under the Drugs and Cosmetics and the FD&C Act. These acts ensure that the drugs and cosmetics sold in the nation meet the prescribed quality standards. These acts are enacted for the welfare of the mortals and guarantee that the drugs and cosmetics that are manufactured, sold and distributed in the nations meet the indispensable necessities of humankind.

CHAPTER TWO

LGBT RIGHTS IN INDIA

Author: Devesh Agarwal, III year of B.A.,LL.B from Apex University, Jaipur.

INTRODUCTION

In India it is not the first time when any gender biasness is show but it is harsh reality of accepting the real things. LGBT is the gender not the other things which is given the phobia to someone. It is high time to discuss about the rights of lgbt. With the time changes are showing in India after the landmark judgment related to homosexuality. Development is going on but we need more clarity to understand this concept because awareness is necessary for everyone. Let's take a look how this started and expand it how.

ABOUT LGBT COMMUNITY

LGBT is not the first time we discussed about it. It is also exist in history as well. But acceptance is come with the later time. It is the new community like others. But, we need a wider and broader view to understand this. It is common like others. LGBT could be a set up that stands for lesbian-gay-bisexual and transgender. LGBT body is mostly determined grouping of lesbian, gay, bisexual and transgender. The word ''homosexual'' has been accustomed show a various cluster or individuals who are smitten or attracted to people of a similar cluster or gender or are In relationship with somebody with a similar gender. it's necessary to acknowledge, however, that completely different teams at intervals the gay community exits, which the term ''gay'' isn't all-encompassing. Transsexual and a few those that are bisexual don't contemplate themselves to be gay. In Sudan, Asian nation, Persia and Republic of Yemen sexual practice remains punishable by ending life beneath Shria law. With the multiplied world media attention on violent act of abuse inflicted on lesbian , gay, bisexual, & transgender person , a vital question before the globe community these days is whether or not gay rights.

PROBLEMS FACED BY LGBT IN INDIA

At the united nation this question is slowly taking center stage. The united nation has been operating with member of states to rejects difference and legislation supported preconception and transphobia. Whereas the denial of human rights for LGBT person Persists throughout the globe these days. LGBT community faces bundle of issues in their day to day life because of that they hide their identity. it's tough for them to Live their life peacefully. The Mass downside long-faced by LGBT community is that voters or individuals of alternative community don't settle for LGBT community equally because of the Changes in their sexual orientation that aren't a part of traditional citizenry. They are facing, discrimination, inequality, Insult in virtually each location, website and place around the world. Individuals mock at them by creating ridiculous comments on their identity, anatomical structure, visual communication and Habits etc. And build them feel awkward and completely different. LGBT community extant with several issues within their day to day life in our society and it becomes tough for them to survive in the society with respect. They are facing Intolerance, variation, state, poverty, lack of care, harassment and threats in society simply because they belonged to homosexual class. LGBT individuals hide their gender by not revealing it at their Abode, simply to feed their family. India should need the acknowledge this they are the part of our society. It should be give equality and respect for their sexuality.

RIGHTS RECOGNIZED BY SUPREME COURT OF INDIA ON LGBT COMMUNITY

The court Realize that section 377 is unconstitutional because it Violate the basic rights of intimacy, identity and autonomy. The Bill State that transgender person can have the proper to self-perceived individuality. This bill Ban discrimination against transgender person in instructional establishments, government agencies, and whereas taking or getting property on rent, good thing about care and victimization public services. It took seventy years or a lot of and virtually two polygonal shape of the long legal journey to scrape down this bygone age law that had become how to harass and exploit all people who didn't follow with the standard binary of sex and Gender. On August 24th , 2017 Indian supreme court gave the country's LGBT community the liberty to soundly categorical their sexual orientation. Therefore, associate individual's sexual orientation is protected beneath the country's right to privacy law.

There is no Hitch that started by Indian government for LGBT community because it is that the duty of each national to respect their community as they're conjointly the humans and an attractive creature of god. Indian Supreme court gave the historical judgment on LGBT community. Supreme Court sanctioned section 377. Navtej Singh Johar & ors. Versus Union of India the Secretary ministry of law and justice is a landmark call of the supreme court of India in 2018 that sanctioned all accordant sex among together with adult, homosexual sex.

Article 21 of Constitution of Indian reads as, "No person shall be deprived of his life or personal liberty except according to a procedure established by law." This text lay out for the defense of life and Sovereignty as a basic right to any or all Residentiary of Republic of India. Supreme Court of Republic of India initiate Section 377 to be in violation of those constitutional rights as right to privacy couldn't avail by the LGBT community members.

<u>REACTION AFTER CHANGES</u>

when this historical judgment of Supreme Court of Republic of India, Republic of India place itself into the list of these virtually a hundred and fifty countries wherever homosexual activity is legal. Section 377 legislating by providing Equivalent basic rights to LGBT community as that alternative national was the primary step towards recognizing the rights of the LGBT community in Republic of India. It is the matter of proud for each national of Republic of India that we tend to are within the support of LGBT community currently. These rights aren't rights that provided direct to LGBT however will be Expound as they're Residential of Republic of India. LGBT community in Republic of India and altogether over the globe deserves to be treated equally with respect and dignity.

<u>CONCLUSION</u>

Each community and Residential of Republic of India have the Rights to be treated equally whether or not they are homosexuals or heterosexuals as a result of every person are creation of god's thus there ought to be no discrimination on the idea of sexual characters. Indian Constitution Permit basic rights to any or all the individuals together with LGBT community. It furnish Right to Right against discrimination, Equality on the idea of sex, Right to Freedom of Speech and Expression ,Right to life, , Right to Privacy and alternative spiritual and cultural rights. As judiciary is in support of LGBT community in India's however undue to worry of law we should always respect them.

CHAPTER THREE

PORTUGUESE LAWS AND CIVIL DISOBEDIENCE MOVEMENT

Author: Riza Rodrigues, LL.M from V.M Salgaocar College of Law, Miramar-Goa

On the 15th of August in the year 1947, our country was finally autonomous and separated from the British. However, whilst the rest of the country was celebrating its independence, Goa was still under foreign Portuguese rule as they established rule and settled in fragmented parts of India. Goa was consequently annexed by the Indian armed forces on the December 19, 1961. Equipped paramilitaries, citizens, the press as well as renowned performers battled for Goa's liberation. The Portuguese were relentlessly persistent to contest India's assertion on its shoreline territory. Worldwide intervention was also unsuccessful to persuade the Portuguese Régime to alter the government's stance.

The times gone by show us that in the year 1492, our state of Goa formed a portion of the domain of Adil Shah. Subsequently, Afonso de Albuquerque occupied Goa devastating Adil Shahs army in collusion with the aid of the Vijayanagar kingdom. Afonso de Albuquerque sought to create a settlement in addition to a navigational abode. Goa remained the center of the Portuguese Empire in the continent of Asia. In those times, farming and cultivation remained the foremost font of revenue for the majority of the populace. A large variety of fruits and vegetables stood cultured commercially in Goa. Trade of a large variety of foreign merchandises prevailed in the State. Precious gems, ceramic ware and fine silks amongst other such luxury goods were made available. It is important to note that foreign trade was running with the assistance of proceeds and profits which were predominantly derived from Goa. The primary goal of the Portuguese administration was conversely trade, and not a coup d'état.

The freedom effort begun rapidly subsequent to the prompting of Mr. Ram Manohar Lohia in 1946. Mr Lohia and a companion Goan Mr Juliao Menezes cavorted a vital part in the freedom movement. The duo lead the way to the civilian defiance undertaking in contradiction of Salazar's authoritarian command over Goa, in addition to leading numerous supplementary activities. Mr. Menezes pursed a degree in medicine in Berlin where he came across Mr Lohia in the campus. The two meet various times and discussed the state of affairs imminent situation in Goa. Thereafter, the twosome came to the conclusion that something has to be done and proceeded to object to the prohibition on municipal assemblies forced on by the prevalent Portuguese régime. This event is categorized as the major civil disobedience movement in rejection of the 435 year antediluvian Portuguese administration.

The Civil Disobedience Movement imparted a sense of boldness among the Goans and reinforced their morality, encouraging copious loyalists to hurdle into the whirlpool of the independence tussle. It captivated all the administrative assemblies and supporter of independence to join political parties such as the Congress party. The National Congress in Goa lingered as the chief radical party during those times. Numerous nationalists gave up their lives. A number of them were extradited to Portugal, Angola and Cabo Verde for extended terms of detention. Mr. Lohia was apprehended by the authorities and consequently arrested which resulted in the movement's actuality to be put down. This incident however encouraged Goans to become more involved in administrative proceedings. Individuals started to consolidating, devising and debating events of national importance. This led to a large number of individuals to pursue and become a part of the struggle which ultimately led to autonomy. The participation of the beginning Indian régime in the struggle for Goa was very low-slung at first. In the meantime Portugal stood as a member of the NATO and the newly formed Indian administration was not prepared clash with a NATO country. After a short time, the Prime Minister of India, Mr. Nehru decided to use their power and strength of the Indian army with complete airborne and navigational provision to combat, and thereafter in fewer than 2 days, Goa was take possession of. The prevailing Governor General of Goa signed the categorical submission. Subsequently, the Assembly approved the 12th Amendment Act which officially assimilated the seized terrains to the Union of India. Goa, Daman and Diu was made a Union Territory.

Soon after liberation, the laws pertinent to the rest of the country were overstretched to Goa. However, the family code laws were retained and are still prevalent in the State. This law has been held in high regard as every person wedded as per the prevalent decree enjoys equivalent property rights. This special code has been in existence for centuries together however legitimate tutelage and knowledge on its numerous articles is still deficient. These laws have been written in the Portuguese language and in the context of the Portuguese language which differs even when translated. The Goan government embarked on an undertaking whereby a version of the civil code has been subtracted from the main body and passed in the assembly as an Act. This Act is known as the Goa, Succession, Special Notaries and Inventory Proceedings Act, 2012. Nevertheless, the Portuguese Civil Code has aided in influencing Goa's broad-based distinctiveness and this imprint must be deliberated upon so that the country can study the law as a model for the country. This lot of decrees contain clutch of exclusive sections like communion of assets, identical property privileges for both genders, in addition to the point that the rules apply unvaryingly to all state residents. The Portuguese Civil Code is a part of Goa's foreign bygone years and was imposed in the formative years of the then Portuguese, and is every so often flaunted by legislators as an example that promises equality and impartiality. The mandate for a uniform civil code is viciously argued, however, the goal of these laws is primarily that of fairness and equality which will only be attained by fortifying a collective bunch of family rules for one and all. Every law has further scope for improvement and needs to adjust to the changings times, our State family laws are not perfect but they are still an excellent model of an advanced group of decrees, Our reformist laws were also given due regard by the Chief Justice of India, Justice Bobde, during the inaugural function of the new structure of the high court of Bombay at Goa. It is said that our Goan law is goal that our constitution makers had envisioned.

The Laws prevalent in the State of Goa are unique, distinct and one of a kind. Implementing and drafting a code that is uniform to the entire country is a far-reaching goal and must be undertaken. The Portuguese Civil Code has been appreciated by researchers, advocates and even Supreme Court judges in their various judgments. However applying a model of our Portuguese Civil Code to that of our country so as to implement and adapt a uniform civil code throughout the country comes with its challenges. Our laws have been regarded as uniform, however in some aspects our laws are stagnant and uneven and partakes few exclusions for diverse religious convictions. On the whole, all groups are enclosed within the Portuguese Civil Code nevertheless the aforementioned must not remain believed as the flawless model as imagined by the legislators.

<u>Author's Biography</u>

Miss. Riza Rodrigues comes from Goa, India. She attended V.M Salgaocar College of Law, where she received her B.A LL.B and then went on to complete an advance degree, an LL.M in the field of Corporate Law, in the same college. During her years at V.M Salgaocar College of Law, she has interned at various establishments. She has also volunteered at various organsitions such as SCAN! (Stop Child Abuse Now), which is nationally recognized NGO, which works relentlessly towards prevention of child abuse in the State of Goa. Miss

Riza Rodrigues has won prestigious prizes while in Law College, most notably the first place in Vis YIMC held in Hong Kong. She is currently a practicing Advocate in High Court, District Court, Trial Courts and revenue courts across the State of Goa, dealing with variety of facets of law such as Civil Law, Criminal Law, Corporate Law, Property Law, Arbitration, Conciliation and Mediation, etc.

CHAPTER FOUR

ENVIRONMENTAL HAZARD: THE CONCEPT OF MASS TORT LITIGATION

Author: Siddharth Singh, V Year of B.A.,LL.B from Amity Law School , sector 125 noida , uttar pradesh.

Introduction

When we talk about India's economic process, it's not surprising that the country became a juggernaut in 30 years. Since the 1991 reforms, capitalism has changed India, with Western and Japanese companies trying to invest their money in the Indian lands. At the same time, the Indian economy despite being one of the world's largest has several loopholes.

The proviso schools will tell you is the immense class split between the rich and poor people. A report by The Times of India expresses that consistently India adds five extremely rich people. A similar report referenced that India has 60% of its kin living on the neediness line. That additionally incorporates the 1/3rd who live in the ghetto regions. Though 10% of India's rich controls 3/4 of its assets.

To accommodate its growing population, urbanization and globalization rose immensely. We see more buildings every day and fewer trees. For example in 2009, when I went to Ranchi, my relative's house used to have a lot of greeneries with trees surrounding the area. It was soothing to walk around those areas. However, when I returned to the city in 2013, I saw that the natural trees were being replaced with concrete ones. In other words, many trees were being cut down to increase the number of buildings.

The example I just gave you was one of many instances where the environment is being affected because of capitalism. We see factories sending their toxic smokes, and without the trees sucking carbon dioxide, breathing air becomes difficult. The smogs we see in Delhi are one of those examples.

As a former humanities student, I read the end of bipolarity in Class 12th Political Science. When I did more digging, I read about how the Chernobyl disaster played a huge role in the downfall of the Soviet Union. The radiation caused by the nuclear power plant has a tremendous impact on Ukraine's environment.

Anyway, Torts also plays a huge role in environmental degradation. In the world of law, torts see how people get injured after a wrongful act has been committed. Taj Trapezium, Bhopal Gas Tragedy, all the M.C. Mehta cases have significant involvement of environmental torts where people and the environment are affected because of the stupidity of mankind. I'll talk about these cases later. For now, I'll first talk about torts and mass torts. And then, I will talk about the environment with these cases.

Definition and examples of Mass Torts

We as a whole know the meaning of torts. For the individuals who are living under the stone, torts mean individuals getting injured because somebody submits an unjust demonstration. Mass torts, then again, imply that a goliath enterprise is at risk for making injury individuals. At the point when an organization submits a "mass misdeed," the individuals who are harmed might have the option to sue the organization and recuperate pay.

For example, accept a drug organization delivers a faulty medication into the commercial center, and that medication is offered to a great many Americans. Patients who were harmed because of the imperfection – say, a defective plan – might have the option to sue the drug organization for hospital expenses identified with their treatment, just as some other misfortunes (for example lost wages, actual agony) originating from their wounds.

Cigarettes

For quite a long time, the tobacco business deceived its clients about the risks of smoking. In 1998, the four biggest tobacco organizations consented to pay $206 billion more than 25 years to state legislatures to repay them for smoking-related Medicaid costs. Cigarette smokers and their survivors keep on recording claims against the tobacco business and a large number of these claims affirm that cigarette organizations wrongfully promote their items to youngsters. Likewise, a huge number of claims are as of now forthcoming against the tobacco business charging that cigarette organizations are deceiving clients about the security of alleged "light" cigarettes.

The Activision Blizzard Case

To highlight more about mass torts, let me bring up the case that I've been researching: The Activision Blizzard Case. Several Employees, especially female employees have accused the aforementioned corporation of sexual harassment, frat boy culture, nepotism, and the death of an employee by suicide. In fret culture. female employees were made to do most of the work while male employees and employers drink and play video games. Rape jokes were also involved in this case. Employees, investors, and even the State of California got involved in this. You can read more about this in my other writings on LA Times, LiveWire, and SOL ADR.

Difference Between Mass Torts and Class Action

1. A mass misdeed claim is like a class activity in that a mass misdeed includes an enormous number of people who have experienced comparative mischief because of a similar improper demonstration; notwithstanding, there is one vital contrast to remember:
2. Mass Tort Lawsuits Are Usually Filed Individually.
3. Every individual who was hurt because of a mass misdeed should record their claim. The legitimate privileges of these people are not naturally secured in the manner in which class individuals' freedoms are in a

class activity. On the off chance that an organization settles the case, those harmed because of the mass misdeed won't get pay except if they have documented their own, individual claims. (Now and again including natural catastrophes, for example, oil slicks, the claim might be documented as a class activity, however, each class part might be needed to submit definite evidence of their singular harms.)

Environmental Cosmos in Mass Torts

Bhopal Gas Tragedy Case

I accept we are on the whole acquainted with the Bhopal Gas Tragedy Case. In December 1984, a lot of MIC spilled in the Union Carbide Factory in Bhopal. It got blended in with Bhopal's outside air, and thus, it turned into a tremendous misfortune. Losses express that 3,000 spirits lost their lives, and 6 lakh individuals were harmed due to breathing in the MIC.

In the aftermath, the already pissed-off victims sued the corporation in Bhopal and even in the United States. They blamed the corporation for their incompetence which led to a severe loss of lives. The parties tried to take this into arbitration but that did not work out. The Indian Government also filed a lawsuit against the Union Carbide Corporation in New York District Court. But the suits of UCC persuaded the court that the case doesn't have any jurisdiction in the US. Since the incident happened in Bhopal, the Indian courts will handle it.

Thrice, the UCC attempted to win the case, and thrice they fail so hard. It's like an angry Russian kid on Minecraft who cried like a volcano after getting IP banned. The UCC tried their hands on Bhopal District Court, only to get slapped hard by the latter by fining them Rs 350 crores of victim's compensation. So they appealed to the Madhya Pradesh High Court, only for them to get roasted by the latter albeit the fine was reduced to Rs 250 crore. So as a last resort, they went to Supreme Court. Well, the last one was epic because the Apex Court game ended them by increasing the compensation to Rs 750 crores ($ 470 million).

The Taj Trapezium

M.C. Mehta, the lover of environmental cases, also filed the case before the Supreme Court. The Taj Mahal is one of the most recognized Seven Wonders in the world. However, MC found out that the Taj's White Marble was turning yellow. He found out that the factories surrounding the monument played a huge role in making the marble yellow. So the Supreme Court decided to assist in preserving the monument's beauty. The factories surrounding the Taj Mahal were ordered to switch to natural gas. Those who fail to comply were ordered to move their factories out the ground zero. If I mean by ground zero, then I mean the Taj Trapezium Zone or TTZ in short.

The industries that fail to follow either of those orders were to shut down and move somewhere else. That's the only option they have, should they want to use coal and coke. The industries must also follow the protocol of recognizing the rights and benefits of the workers. The latter must be allowed to work in the relocated areas. They must also be given wages in full amount as well as shifting bonuses.

MC Mehta v. Kamal Nath and Ors.

In this judgment, the court put corrupting in the portrayal of typical off track and conveyed that dirtying the climate is an offense submitted against the entire area.

The Court was besides of the view that "the individual who is committed for harming the science and climate might be compelled to pay model harms in like the way so that such honor might display to go probably as a framework for others to keep them away from repeating a near botch". Regardless, the Court detached between fine and praiseworthy harm by saying that both are the consequences of various kinds of musings. The Court reiterated that its forces are not restricted and as expected it can yield harms through PIL's and writs under Art. 32.

Bandhua Mukti Morcha v. Association Of India

This was a milestone judgment because of the way that in this judgment the Hon'ble Supreme Court expressed that "the force of the court under Article 32 which manages right to established cures isn't restricted distinctly with giving bearings, rules or writ to implement principal freedoms however it puts a commitment on the Court to check whether the crucial privileges of individuals are secured or not".

<u>Absolute and Strict Liability</u>

Absolute Liability for the damage brought about by industry occupied with unsafe and intrinsically hazardous exercises is a recently figured teaching liberated from the exemptions for the severe risk rule in England. The Indian principle was advanced in MC Mehta v. Association of India, which was prominently known as the Oleum gas spill case. It was public interest prosecution under Article 32 of the Indian constitution.

Misdeed law likewise establishes the Doctrine of Strict Liability. Severe obligation implies that an individual needs to show that he/she didn't deliberately partake in the said episode because of their behavior. The

Doctrine of Strict Liability is otherwise called obligation without issue. An individual who brings himself dangers through his careless activities isn't granted harm.

The disadvantage of this is that the weight of verification lays on the shoulders of the offended party. In natural contamination-related cases, it turns out to be exceptionally difficult to demonstrate and present proof against the respondents. This teaching was discussed exhaustively on account of Rylands v. Fletcher(1868).

Role of Nuisance

As per Stephen, aggravation is anything done to the hurt or disturbance of the apartments of another, or of the grounds, one which doesn't add up to intrude.

As indicated by almond, irritation comprises in causing or permitting to cause without legal avocation, the break of any harmful thing from one's property or from anyplace into land possessing the offended party, like water, smoke, gas, heat, power, and so forth

For instance, a singular plants a tree in his territory yet the parts of the tree are spreading to the next's property this would add up to the demonstration of disturbance.

Types of Nuisance

Public Nuisance is a preposterously, outlandishly, or unlawful obstruction with a right that is shared by all individuals from people in general. A public annoyance is a demonstration that influences the overall population or a critical part of it, and it should encroach on freedoms that individuals from the local area may some way or another have.

Accordingly, acts that truly meddle with the wellbeing, security, solace, or accommodation of the public by and large or which will in general corrupt public ethics have consistently been viewed as a public annoyance. For instance, blocking a public way by burrowing a channel. The continuing exchange causes a hostile smell.

Private Nuisance happens when someone else meddles with an individual's utilization or satisfaction in his property. It might likewise make hurt the landowner by genuinely hurting his property or meddling with his delight in it. Rather than public aggravation, private irritation risks a singular's utilization or satisfaction in property, instead of people in general or society.

There are two sorts of private annoyance for example Harm to the property and Physical inconvenience.

Harm to the property – Any sensible injury to the property will do the trick to help a case for harm on account of aggravation regarding the property. In the case of property harm, any sensible hurt will get the job done to legitimize activity. Assembling plants, chains, and different wellsprings of this class of inconveniences might be to be faulted.

Actual Discomfort-There is two necessities that should be met in an aggravation suit getting from actual misery. In the first place, the outsider's utilization ought to be outside of the normal flow of one party's pleasure, and second, the inconvenience ought to be sufficiently serious to influence an individual locally, and people ought not to have the option to endure or persevere through the enjoyment.

Conclusion

Around then, India was likewise encountering enormous modern switches that prompted the setting around of many organizations that were occupied with risky substances.

Subsequently, it is protected to decipher that the development of misdeed law corresponding to natural contamination has cleared a pathway for the individuals who are hurt by something similar to acquire remuneration. It has additionally forewarned organizations occupied with perilous substances towards their risk. This advancement has cleared a path for better organization of equity.

Further advancement of the standard of Absolute Liability (the main part that is one of a kind to the requirements of India and has not been embraced from English law) requests more noteworthy responsibility and secures freedoms through cure/pay. It is acknowledged that danger to one's life is terrible wrongdoing and can't be pardoned under any conditions.

Eventually, it could be said that, in spite of the fact that there is a lack of misdeed and particularly ecological misdeeds prosecution in India, the new advancements in the beyond thirty years have been good. In the wake of joining misdeed law with freedoms under the constitution and broadening the implementation under Art. 32, it is currently simpler for the overall population to get a cure when contrasted with the situation before MC Mehta. Likewise, with the development of bodies like the National Green Tribunal (NGT) and Forest Survey of India, keeping a mind the issues of ecological damages and corruption has become exceptionally productive and works of these bodies are additionally useful in expanding the attention to the overall population. By and large, the viability of cure with the appearance of Deep-Pocket hypothesis had upset climate identified with misdeed suit in India.

Author's Biography

My name is Siddharth Singh and I'm a 5th Year Law Student currently studying at Amity Law School, NoidaMy hometown is Varanasi and I have an interest in politics. I wrote an article regarding the issues of domestic violence on the platform known as Youth Ki Awaaz. I have also participated in various events within and outside my college like moot courts, mock parliaments, etc. Because my family is of the political background, I have been active in political and social events like Indian Youth Congress, Sunbeam Varna Sabha, NCC, etc. As a social worker, I have participated in every social activities in Varanasi. Helping the weaker sections of the society has become a major interest of mine. In the legal sphere, I have learned how to draft legal notice, affidavit, bail petitions through internships. I also have an interests in researching topics that are related to Code of Civil Procedure and the Hindu Marriage Act. My aim in this is to become self sufficient and at the same time, be politically active so that I could help the people of not only my constituency but also my country. I hope you enjoy reading my article and I'm keen on listening to your opinion.

CHAPTER FIVE

THROUGH THE 'FILTERS' OF SOCIAL MEDIA: ANALYSING ITS AUTHENTICITY IN THE CONTEMPORARY WORLD

Author: Prerna Deep, Law Clerk-cum-Research Assistant under Hon'ble Justice at the Supreme Court of India.

Co-author: Shruti Kirti, Assistant Editor at Publications Division, Ministry of Information & Broadcasting.

Introduction

Social media with its infinite appearances, provides social support in faster dissemination of information. It was aimed at strengthening the bond of connecting families and friends. It was also bridging people from different horizons and creating a sense of belongingness in them. The 'new self' that became the talk of the social media town, was a content, flourishing, and almost envy-inducing self, living its best life. People began sharing their ideas, which was often rebuked as a deceptive outward guise. The filtered content being shared often created a distorted sense of reality, which sprung a new debate of falsehood and deceit.

While social media provides a site for people to fraternise and express their views, this article awakens the reader about the ascent of social media with its multiple-layered process and how it is deeply intertwined with legal consequences and censorship.

Blurring lines between Reel and Real

The obsessive dependence on social media has affected the psychological and physiological health of mankind. According to a research conducted by Statista, in 2018, 2.62 billion people were spending a portion of their day scrolling and using social media.[1] It emerges as a new touchstone to focus on fulfilling an 'accomplished' life virtually. The portrait of this unblemished day can be a mere pretence to share with the world. The critical question is the price one pays for all this façade. While the direct consequences may not be something that one notes in the diary, the psychological aftermaths are often understated and misunderstood.

Levi-Beiz and Turel[2] coined the term "Facebook-self" for the false personalities created by netizens to display themselves on social media. Their study further shows a direct correlation between an increase in the number of feigned online personalities, with a decline in self-esteem and authenticity in real life. These influencers often try to overcompensate for their imperfect life through an impeccable portrayal of self. Thus, these may be rightly called as 'hyper-realities' and therefore do not serve the purpose they claim to aim.

Social media often augments one's vulnerabilities and insecurities, becoming an indicator of anxiety. A research conducted by Bevan, Gomez, Sparks [3] suggested 'age groups 18-70 Facebook users have more stress and lesser quality of life'. The selfie realm has highlighted the concerns regarding representation of a 'perfect' face and body image, and a culture where everyone needs to follow certain principles in order to be trending.

For example, the Blue Whale challenge (2016) lured teenagers to pursue self-harm activities and kill themselves as the final task. Not only does such competitiveness tend to suppress one's morale concerning how they should act and react, it also makes them believe that they are a part of a universal significance beyond their own limited lives. This façade promises a pretentious acceptance by the world wide web, but in reality, no one enters or leaves it.

Social Media as a Business Model

An underrated dimension of social media that remains unnoticed is that it works well as a successful business model. This is a 24*7 running business market, and therefore it mints financial profit continuously. While laws in other domains are easier to regulate in the country, the omnipresence of this media and the fluidity that accompanies it makes social media regulations complicated and controversial. The internet market of India is on a constant rise and is currently placed in the top three of the world with around 700 million internet users.[4] As Claypoole suggests, "much of the business model development for social media sites is designed to coerce, cajole, trick, taunt, or tease us into revealing more information about our lives and our thoughts and opinions."[5]

There are legal breaches in terms of intellectual property laws, and subverting business and consumer laws.[6] There have been attempts in the past by the government trying to censor the media or create guidelines to prevent these from happening, but the global nature of social media makes it challenging.

The Marxist[7] tendency of this capitalist world where money making is the primary aim, remains at work while developing the social media websites. This fundamental rule appears to be applied by various platforms to cater their own purpose, which have their own target audience. Snapchat, for example, emerged as an idea when someone sent a personal photo to a wrong contact. It gave birth to self-destructing snaps and delete options for messages from one end in Telegram and WhatsApp, and recently introduced Instagram's vanishing mode. Internet users are inclined to believe that numerous websites which also save their personal passwords, and information about all the transactions, make their jobs of writing 16-digit card details easy, but they fail to discern the fraud that can wipe them off their life's savings.

Cyber Bullying

"Commanding the trend represents a relatively novel and increasingly dangerous means of persuasion within social media."[8] The internet users get to choose what to post and show the world about themselves, they also choose what to see and what part of information to accept as the ultimate truth. Prier concludes that "the adaptation of social media as a tool of modern warfare should not be surprising."[9]

Social media can facilitate many cybercrimes, including cyber-bullying. We can easily access where or with whom someone stayed, what they ate and did, at that very instant. This oversharing of rapid information leads to the knowledge of someone at a vulnerable position (as a data directory for criminals to find the easiest of targets), or sometimes reveals their identity which was supposed to be kept confidential. In addition, the cyber-bullying aspect of social media gets far too little recognition than it deserves.[10] Unfortunately, it has become a common occurrence to give women rape and murder threats on online platforms, even during arguments that are frivolous; however, if the same threats were given in the real world than virtual, it would be profoundly taken with greater sensitivity and responsibility. While the authorities might not take intimidating remarks on social media as par with the non-virtual ones, its effect on victims is extreme[11]. It often leads to women feeling terrorised within their safe space, causing extreme distress, and in some rather unfortunate events, can also push towards suicidal attempts.

This gap is an oversight by the legal and policing system, and while there exists a cybercrime cell for the same, there is a need for better-implemented regulations, sensitisation, and censorship of the content that is often violent and inflammatory towards vulnerable and marginalised sections of the society.

Conclusion

Recent global controversies exemplify that the central objective of social media often gets deviated when a positive reaction to it also brings hatred and segregation amongst people. It simultaneously becomes a tool that unites as well as divides groups. The broadcasting of the George Floyd incident rightly angered the world against the greatly troubling hate crime-racism; then it regrettably divided Indians on whether they recognise casteism in their own country or not. Social media coerces one to choose one of the extreme stances, where normalcy of mistakes are made instantaneously unacceptable and become an object of mockery. Users discuss and share their opinions on their social media, but those are not without prejudices or stereotypes.

At last, social media is a garden full of roses that hides its thorns so ornately, that one tends to believe they do not exist at all. The unreliability of social networks with its silhouettes not only ascertains that one needs to be cautious in its usage, but also confirms that it subconsciously alters behaviour and life choices, and still thrives to find light at the end of the tunnel by making monetary benefits out of it.

Authors' Biography

Prerna Deep

Prerna Deep is the recipient of British Council GREAT Scholarship (2019) for pursuing LLM in Criminal Law and Criminal Justice at the University of Edinburgh. She is currently working as a Law Clerk-cum-Research-Assistant under Hon'ble Justice of Supreme Court of India. She holds LL.B. from Campus Law Centre, University of Delhi and English Honours from Miranda House, University of Delhi. As an avid reader and writer, Prerna has authored several Nationally and Internationally published research papers and articles.

Shruti Kirti

Shruti Kirti is a Masters in English Literature from the University of Delhi, India; currently working as an Assistant Editor in Publications Division, Ministry of Information and Broadcasting, Government of India. Her areas of interest include media studies, post-colonial literature, comparative literature, and socio-cultural research.

CHAPTER SIX

TRADE DRESS PROTECTION- COMPARATIVE STUDY OF US AND INDIAN POSITION

Author: Arya Sudhir Nikam, III year of B.A.,LL.B(Hons.) From Maharashtra National Law University, Mumbai.

Trade Dress denotes the outward aspect of items, such as packaging, form, and colour combination, that can be registered or protected by rivals in terms of their company and services. It assists consumers in identifying and distinguishing the product from others. It also aids an ignorant buyer in differentiating a product based on its packaging. The US was the first to recognise this notion. The new Trade Marks Act 1999 went into effect in September 2003 and is primarily based on the English Trademark Act, 1994, which acknowledged the notion of trade dress along the lines of The Lanham Act.

Trade Dress protection is intended to shield customers against product packaging or look that is designed to compete with other items. It stops customers from purchasing a goods under the mistaken notion that it belongs to someone else. The major goal is also to keep goods and services from being copied. It should stand out from the crowd. It should not cause misunderstanding in the minds of customers so that there is no unfair usage of that goods.

Trade Dress Essentials

1. Shape, size, colour, texture, product arrangement, and so on are all examples.

2. A product's packaging is likely to be one-of-a-kind.

3. The colour of the product also contributes to its individual personality.

India's Trade Dress Protection Act

Under the Trademark Act of 1999, there is no explicit definition of trade dress in India. However, owing to changes in intellectual property laws, a new Amendment recognised trade dress protection under Section 2 of the Trademark Act through a revised definition of a trademark. Trade dress is governed by unfair competition laws. Both state and federal laws ban enterprises from impersonating or duplicating one another.

According to Section 2 of the Trademark Act, a trademark is a graphical representation and overall look of a product that differentiates one person's products and services from those of others, such as the form of items, their packaging, and colour combination. In addition, the terms "package" and "Mark" are defined in this section.Prior to 2003, Indian courts began to recognise the idea of trade dress.

The new Indian law definition of a trademark includes all of the components of trade dress under US law. Trade dress as a notion might encompass the design of a magazine cover page, the visual look of a lamp, the design of sports shoes, and so on.

A generic notion or a creative concept, on the other hand, cannot be protected as a trade dress. Indian courts have granted trade dress protection through a common law remedy known as "passing off" (enforcement against an unauthorised use).

The clause of Section 9(3) of the Trademarks Act 1999 states the form of products registration of the trademark.According to Section 9(3) of the Trademark Act of 1999, a mark may only be registered if it does not include:

A) A natural form of a product.

B) A form that adds significant value to the product.

This demonstrates the Doctrine of Functionality (which forbids a party from getting trade dress in a product's functional element), which is recognised under Indian Trademark Law. Distinctiveness is also an important factor in Trademark and Trade Dress, which indicates that a trade dress must be distinctive, i.e. easily recognised by customers. Trademark protection is provided for both registered and unregistered trademarks, as is trade dress protection.Many times, courts have made judgements based on a product's trade dress aspect. Indian judicial decisions have likewise identified trade dress as an important part of intellectual property protection. The Indian judiciary has recognised trade dress aspects such as product form, colour combination, and packaging.

Trade Dress Protection in the United States

Trade dress protection is specified in the United States under Section 43(a) of the Lanham Act, which states that trade dress is defined as the whole look of the goods, which may include size, form, colour combination, and so on. It is open to both registered and unregistered trade dress (the symbol, word etc. used by the company which is registered under the Trademarks Act 1999 is known as registered trademark and any symbol, word etc. used by the company but is not registered is know as unregistered trademark). The trade dress must be original, exceptional, or generally recognised by the public in order to be protected.

Section 43(a) of the Lanham Act prohibits civil aviation from using any word or combination of words, phrase, name, symbol, or other identifier linked with another's goods that causes confusion. This legislation does not cover a product's functional features.

Under US law, distinctiveness might be general, descriptive, suggestive, arbitrary, or whimsical. Generic marks cannot be trademarked since all merchants should be able to use such phrases to describe their items while competing with customers.

Trade Dress is significant because it prevents businesses from engaging in unethical acts. Section 43(a) of the Lanham Act prohibits civil aviation from using any word or combination of words, phrase, name, symbol, or other identifier linked with another's goods that causes confusion.

This legislation does not cover a product's functional features.

Under US law, distinctiveness might be general, descriptive, suggestive, arbitrary, or whimsical. Generic marks cannot be trademarked since all merchants should be able to use such phrases to describe their items while competing with customers. Trade Dress is significant because it prevents businesses from engaging in unethical acts.In the United States, the two most important criteria for trade dress protection are distinctiveness and non-functionality. This criterion must be followed for trade Dress protection; otherwise, compensation should be paid to the affected party.

If a plaintiff files a claim for infringement, he or she must demonstrate the following three elements:

i) The plaintiff has a distinctive trade dress in a flawless design or mix of features.

ii) Confusion is created by the suspected trade dress.

iii) If the defendant's trade dress is not registered, the plaintiff must establish that it is not functioning. If it is registered, the defendant bears the burden of demonstrating functioning.The third argument raised above is intriguing, and in order to fulfil it, the trade dress for protection must not be practical. The arrangement of forms, patterns, and colours leaves no doubt in the minds of the clients.

If the foregoing three trade dress components are satisfied, there are two remedies available:

-Suspension of proceedings (the Courts order to stop one party from infringing trade dress of another party)

-Financial Losses (compensation for loss suffered by the injured party).

The regulations governing trade dress protection in both of these countries are nearly identical. One distinction between US trade dress and Indian trade dress is that in the US, trade dress is registered by meeting specific standards, however in India, the Trademarks Act does not recognise the phrase trade dress, hence it is not protected. Certain characteristics of the goods, such as a colour combination, form, and so on, can be registered. The United States has well-established trade dress protection, but India is slowly making headway in recognising trade dress protection. However, both nations have identical trade dress protection.

Trade Dress protection can also be offered for the shape of a soft drink container, the shape of furniture, or the design of the showroom. Some well-known examples of trade dress include the shape of a Coca-Cola bottle and the grills of a Rolls-Royce car. With more competitors, trade dress offers a new venue for securing the aspect of distinctiveness. Even illiterate customers can tell the difference between products based on their packaging. The colour of a product also provides it with a distinct identity.

It is mostly concerned with the product's look. It differs from a trademark in that a trademark deals with words, logos, slogans, emblems, and so on that are fixed on a product in order to distinguish it from another.The look of the goods to identify the maker is referred to as trade dress. Under common law, trade dress can be protected by passing off, which protects a company's goodwill.

CHAPTER SEVEN

LEGAL OUTLOOK ON SPACE TOURISM

Author: R. Rebecca Vasanthini Percy, B.Com.,LL.B(Hons.) From The Tamil Nadu Dr Ambedkar Law University, School of Excellence in Law.

Introduction

Human beings have always craved for many things right from their cradlebed till their deathbed. Desires and cravings are never ending. In the olden days, humans desired to get communication and transportation very easily without getting harnessed so this desire let to the invention of telephones, mobiles, train, carts, television etc. After the surfacing of technology and invention of many new things, in the current scenario human beings are blessed with all types of resources and equipments and each and every individual right from the time they get up from the bed till they go to sleep, they can utilise all types of contrivance available in the society. When the power of invention and advancement of technology grew, the never ending satisfaction of human desires sprung up. We people tend to go to different sates, countries and continents to explore and to enjoy new things but what's more interesting and great above all these things was thought by many of us and after going to world tour we feel like okay fine let's start exploring what's beyond the Earth. One such craving of mankind is to explore the space and to go for space tourism.

Human race travelling to space and experiencing it either directly or indirectly is termed as space tourism. It is catalogued into three dimensions namely,

1. Suborbital
2. Orbital
3. Lunar space tourism

In the present scenario it is quite evident that already seven individuals have booked for a space tourism and had gone for a vacation for their personal pleasure and leisure. Presently, the Treaty on Principles Governing the Activities of States in the Exploration and Use of Outer Space, including the Moon and Other Celestial Bodies ("Outer Space Treaty"), the United Nations Committee on the Peaceful Uses of Outer Space ("UN COPUS"), the Convention on International Civil Aviation ("Chicago Convention"), etc. governs the space tourism with their relevant provisions.

<u>**History of Space Tourism**</u>

In 1957, Sputnik I was launched fruitfully after which the Soviet Union wanted to capture the space race first and to lead it. Likewise, in April 1961, Soviet cosmonaut Yuri Gagarin became the first man to go to space. A 108 minute orbital flight was made by Gagarin aboard the Vostok 1 spacecraft. Astronaut Alan Shepard in May 1961 became the first U.S. citizen to go to space. In 1960s human spaceflight was proven and in 1970s the concept of space tourism emerged. In 1980s non- government astronauts went to space and this space mission named space shuttle program was a success as 135 missions were launched and 355 people managed to go to space.

From 1990s again the concept of space tourism reappeared. Space Adventures Ltd. became the first company to take private consumers to space when they were interested in 1998. The second striking space tourism company was XCOR Aerospace in the year 1999. The ultimate motive of these companies was that money should not be the primary hindrance in getting into space and the customers whom they took to space have made tremendous wealth in the dot com bubble and tried to buy places in the space. There were six notable private and wealthy citizens who went to space. They are:

1. In 2002: A South African computer millionaire named Mark Shuttleworth went to space

2. In 2005: An American sensor hardware millionaire Gregory Olson went to space

3. In 2006: An Iranian-American software millionaire Anousheh Ansari took off to space

4. In 2007: A Hungarian-American software billionaire Charles Simonyi went to space and he again visited in 2009

5. In 2008: A British-American video-game millionaire Richard Garriott went for a vacation to space and

6. In 2009: A Canadian billionaire artist Guy Laliberté landed in space.

The emergence of commercial space tourism industry took place from 2010 onwards.

Space tourism in India

The space affairs in India are carried on in a rapid manner even though there is a huge lacuna in the space legislations. The space work is effectively carried on by ISRO. Chandrayan-I is the lodestar in the space activities undertaken by India. A space tourism system should have the following requisite elements:

1. Ample number of windows and place to fly must be there in the space vehicle which carry the passengers.

2. The acceleration level should be kept lower than 3G due to the medical curtailment.

3. The space tour should be limited to several hours only to avoid space illness.

4. Proper health check-ups must be undergone by each passenger before the tour.

5. It must be vital to meet the demand price figures.

An example complying with all the necessary requirements in the space tourism system was accomplished by Kawasaki and Fuji Heavy Industries in 1994.

Relation between Space tour and Insurance

In today's world, as how humans go from one country to another country In flight it has become a common travel in space too. Since the travelling in space has become more frequent and common its high time that the insurance companies insure the passengers against any unforeseen event. It is indeed a good time to buy and have insurance for the spacecraft as market conditions are favouring with premium rates declining and the availability of three- four times of the demand.

Conclusion

Presently, space tours are emerging in nature but how far can this be firmly established in a country like India where there is no body of rules and laws to enforce the space legislation is a big question mark. Many Indian ministries have come up with thought provoking schemes to support this space tourism system in our country. Based on how competitive will this industry grow and how far it will be affordable to all the individuals present in the country, our country is still making a decision and very sooner or later they will be giving some positive outputs regarding the same. Hence its high time that India also develops this space adventure along with the other neighbouring countries and enforce laws and rules accordingly thereby fulfilling the wishes of many people in the country and also our country should take necessary measures to keep the fares at an affordable price thereby allowing every citizen of our country to get an experience of how the space looks like and to enjoy the glimpse of it.

ROLE OF MEDIA AND PRESS IN THE PANDEMIC COVID -19: A LEGAL PERSPECTIVE

Author: Vaishnavi Nimje, III year of B.B.A.,LL.B from Symbiosis Law School, Nagpur.

INTRODUCTION

Media and society are the units which are closely related to each other. The in-depth impact of media on society can be simply be seen. Media reflects our society, how it works and what it constitutes. With the advancement in technological space, our society has conjointly discovered the enlargement within the thoughts and ideas of individuals. Each single invention ranging from the machine to the most recent smartphones our society has accepted it. Earlier individuals used to communicate things with the assistance of sketch and print forms however as time passes the medium became a lot of advanced. Nowadays individuals are just simply a click far from any and each info that's out there on the web. There are numerous sorts of media that facilitate to tell, educate and entertain our society. Media are often in print kind that's through newspapers, books, magazines etc.

Media includes an electronic kind for spreading information that is one amongst the foremost used media of mass communication. With the assistance of radio and television, listeners and viewers not only get updated however it conjointly creates an understanding of current happenings. Radio being an audio medium helps in distributive information to each nook and corner of our country. Radio has conjointly contended a significant role in making a platform for imagination. The reach of this audio medium isn't solely restricted to urban areas however it's lined a large vary even to the remote areas of our country. Initially, TV in our country was introduced for education purpose. However later as time passed the objective of educating people turned into imparting information and entertaining masses. Nowadays TV has become a very important part of our existence. It covers a massive section of programs like daily soaps, news, movies, reality shows, sports, forecast, non secular programs, music etc.

Social media is turning into one amongst the foremost standard and most accessed media of communication of late. The social media act as an umbrella that constitutes a range of fascinating options that have our life terribly easier. options of tagging friends, location sharing, pic and video uploads, message chatting, video vocation, looking out friends etc have created our life a lot of participating.

CONSTITUTIONAL PROVISIONS FOR MEDIA

Media of mass communication are an important part of the fashionable society. They're conjointly terribly powerful systems that influence the society. At a particular level media influences this and may conjointly influence the longer term of the society. Mass media have the ability to form or undo governments. Thus it's clear that mass media are quite powerful.

However the exercise of power by the media gets regulated and controlled by the assorted laws and rules enacted from time to time. In an authoritarian type of governance, the operating of the media is restricted and controlled to a good extent. Mass media get pleasure from sure freedom. However the Constitution imposes sure cheap restrictions. There are unit laws that regulate the functioning of mass media in Asian country. Media laws in Asian country have an extended history right from British rule. The govt enacted many rules and laws in Asian country to preserve in rule. After independence, a lot of laws are enacted and therefore the recent ones amended became the advantage for the society. The Indian Constitution doesn't give freedom for media one by one.

However there's an indirect provision for media freedom. It gets derived from Article 19(1) (a). This text guarantees freedom of speech and expression. the liberty of mass media comes indirectly from this text. Our Constitution conjointly lays down some restrictions within the type of Article 19(2). concerning the problem of freedom of speech, Dr. B. R. Ambedkar explained the position as follows:

"The press (or the mass media) has no special right that don't seem to be to be to or that don't seem to be to be exercised by the national in his individual capability. "The editor of a Press or the manager square measure all voters and, therefore, once they favour to represent any newspapers, they simply sweat their right of expression and in my judgement no special mention is important of the liberty of Press the least bit." Article nineteen of the Indian constitution lays down, " Justice Mudholkar, a Supreme Court choose same throughout Emergency (1975-77), "Pre-censorship, prohibition on import of written and revealed material, inserting a ban on printing and commercial enterprise material of a mere nature, tight security from the press or restriction which might quantity to an indirect curb on free circulation of a newspaper or category of newspaper ought to confine itself have all been command to be unhealthy in law."

Only few countries just like the USA have ensured freedom of media in a very direct manner. In India, abundant legislation has been enacted during this direction. Most governments feel that they need the correct to enact such Acts and Laws with a read towards limiting the liberty of expression within the interest if the state, with relevance friendly relations with foreign states, with relevance public order, with relevance decency or morality, or in reference to contempt of court, defamation, or incitement of offence.

<u>PRESENT SCENARIO - COVID 19</u>

Now talking regarding this scenario, The Covid-19 pandemic is disrupting each trade. For the media sector, coronavirus creates each opportunities and challenges. On one hand, social distancing has diode to a spike in at-home media consumption, and growing numbers square measure turning to news suppliers for timely and trustworthy info on the crisis. At constant time, a number of the foremost valuable broadcast content—such as live sports—is being deferred or off, resulting in outlay reallocations by advertisers and a resultant come by financial gain for media firms. this disruption is also unprecedent, however the media trade has been perpendicular persistently before.

Since the flip of the century, conversion of content, the increase of social media and acceleration in mobile consumption have all forced changes to the manner media firms legalise content. The several considerations related to the COVID-19 crisis: unequipped public health systems, policies to combat the pandemic, and therefore the lack of designing and support to the vulnerable sections. These problems demand serious examination, however the thought of media, exclusion some valiant exceptions, looks to be forgetting its democratic role.

The vilification of migrant labourers and a minority community while failing to critique the dearth of measures to assist these sections influence the crisis is a vital such indicator. The media, however, has worries associated with its own economic scenario. Medium, especially, is handling a resource crunch, dwindling advertisements, and worries of reduction in circulation and audience. With considerations of job security, inadequate resource support, and abuses sweet-faced by the police, several journalists square measure swing their health at stake to hide the COVID-19 scenario. Some media homes have already begun cutting wages; extension within the imprisonment will produce a replacement crisis in Indian journalism.

The role of larger media as determined throughout the pandemic, however, isn't Associate in Nursing nightlong shift. it's been visible currently. The media has seen extraordinary growth throughout the last 3 decades, and Asian nation has become one amongst the most important media markets within the world. The media has become a tool of information and sensationalism. Some newscast channels see a Chinese conspiracy within the unfold of COVID-19. In such a "positive" atmosphere, the news associated with labourers' mass exodus and therefore the markaz was largely given thanks to its sensational price. truth scenario wouldn't have gained attention within the initial place, if not for the ground-level reports by the committed journalists and social media coverage. The Janata curfew declared on 22nd March was unsuccessful as folks came out on the streets within the evening, clapping, banging utensils, shouting non secular slogans, and processing univalve shells, as if they may defeat COVID-19 with a show of such masculinity. Social distancing was forgotten.

Later, folks were once more asked to change off residential lights for 9 minutes and lightweight a candle or diya in their balconies. will the virus extremely be eradicated by chants of "go corona?" However, the media became a locality of this "festivity". These exercises were lapped up by a majority of the fourth estate, because it sells the massive spectacle—a hyper real experience—and accepts the obeisance of a "supreme authority" at the side of an outsized range of voters. The trivialisation of the crisis and a harmful "positivity" is ruling the media. COVID-19 may be a serious threat to the state and thus several rational measures and "honest conversations" should be expected from the govt, that can't be on the far side the crucial radio detection and ranging of journalism. the govt has created a chief Minister's national help and Relief in Emergency things (PM-CARES) Fund to combat the pandemic and plenty of business firms and customary folks have contributed to the present fund.

Moreover, media may carry videos of the victorious treatment cases and therefore the encouraging words of medical practitioners concerned in activity the illness for public respite. Running interviews of psychotherapists and psychological feature speakers might alleviate the discomposed public mind.

Since people are in self-quarantine at this hour of crisis with the government's call of total imprisonment a minimum of for per week currently, contents associated with self-introspection, happiness and family relationships among others might charm to the folk. With the predominance of stories and knowledge relating coronavirus, breaking the monotony additionally needs providing some refreshing materials to entertain the audience. In doing this, media need to cater to the interests of metameric audience – kids, youths and therefore the aged.

<u>CONCLUSION</u>

Unimportant and irrelevant news, that sometimes haven't any importance are given priority and thanks to a reason or the opposite, they catch on the minds of the viewers and in this ways many an times, important political, economical and sociological news get neglected and gradually, lose their importance! No doubt, media has played significant role in making world a worldwide village and to scale back the communication gaps amongst the people living within the far areas but unfortunately, media lately has become a commercialized sector, eying the news which are hot and good at selling. The goal is to realize the TV rating points.

I believe, if the media identifies its responsibility and work sincerely and honestly, then it can function an excellent force in building the State.

Author's Biography

Future Lawyer and a lifelong humanitarian.

'Work Smarter not Harder' is what I believe.

I am pleased to introduce myself as Vaishnavi Nimje. I am currently pursuing BBA LL.B from Symbiosis Law School, Nagpur. I believe myself as a visionary and strategical person who is mainly foucused on problem solving with a view of learning passively.

I am confident that my skillset, competitive edge, giving attention to detail, and passion for law will largely contribute in me achieving these career goals.

Apart from this, I am an active member of an organisation called Junior Chamber International (JCI) . Last year, where COVID hit all of us really hard, I being 'Vice President Community' organised many programs like Vaccination Drive, Blood Donation Camp, Pet Pooja (Food Distribution Drive) etc.

This year, I have been proudly nominated as Secretary of JCI Nagvidarbha. I will give my best to this organisation. I will make sure that I learn and grow maximum as an individual.

CHAPTER NINE

METAVERSE – IPR EQUIVALENCY

Author: Ashish Gupta, LL.M(IPR) from Gujarat National Law University, Gandhinagar

Introduction

Facebook recently rebranded as Meta, making it a multinational technology company which focused on the future, which can be understood from the Greek translation of the term 'meta', which is 'beyond' or 'after'. The popular name of Metaverse being associated with Facebook and its founder Mark Zuckerberg is a different concept of a virtual world. Meta will enable its users to make avatars on Metaverse in order to socialise in an alternate realm or reality. This proves as an opportunity for many IP owners who have a certain brand associated with a distinguishable copyright or trademark, and can use this platform to enhance their reach to people who are invested in making a digital world presence as opposed to in real life and are yet to come across their brands.

IP Issues

However, as easy it is for the IP owners to increase their presence in Metaverse, if any IP owner is not aware of this platform, they run the risk of unauthorized use of their IP, or in a worst-case scenario, the risk of unregistered IP to be used in Metaverse by any user who makes commercial use of it. Unauthorized use of IPs such as Trademarks in games in fictional mode is an already existing precedent, as seen in the case of E.S.S. Entertainment 2000, Inc. V. Rock Star Videos, Inc., wherein the renowned video game GTA used the banners of a club in their game without acquiring appropriate licenses and permissions. Hence, the establishment of Metaverse, which is going to be booming as we further stray away from real life, is a wake-up call for many IP owners to register their IPs, and then further grant licenses for authorized use of it so that they have economic benefits from Metaverse.

Solution

It is critical for every party interested in experimenting in the metaverse today to create explicit IP licence agreements with the metaverse platform provider. Typical terms such as term, area, and royalty rates are crucial in any IP licence, but the scope of the licence should be given special consideration. It is critical to scope the IP licence to accommodate for broad use and predict future uses.

Without mutually granted IP rights, a brand owner may find themselves in a scenario where they are granted certain rights to a digital product but are unable to exploit those rights in the future.

Obtaining registered rights through an old-school strategy to prohibiting unauthorised use of a brand, has its place, but it may not be sufficient in all instances — notably in the metaverse. By establishing usage limitations, brands can reduce the risk of reputational damage caused by unintended brand connotations.

Recognition of Law

Another grey area regarding the IPR regime in relation to the Metaverse is that, what laws will be applicable on the virtual world platform, and who will be the authority to be approached for any dispute relating such unauthorized use of IP. It is ideal that Meta or Metaverse setup their own guidelines for them to take cognizance of any violation, and that laws which are applicable on the user in real life, be applicable on any violation. But it remains to be seen, as what laws will Metaverse adhere to, and how stringent those regulations are to make sure IP owners are not compromised by unauthorized use.

The metaverse is code at its core: ones and zeros covered with incomprehensibly enormous amounts of data. The programmer(s) put in a lot of time and effort to create software. Because the main objective of software is to make processes easier, it is critical to value the work's creation and safeguard it in the name of the creator. It is to be understood that every aspect of metaverse is essentially has its roots in real life IP of different people. Engineers coding a certain unique way are making avatars, are using clothes of a certain idea, which will be someone else's IP, or have a look or voice of a distinct or a famous personality which could be an IP of that person.

Section 2 (ffc) of the Copyright Act 1957, which defines "computer programme" as "a set of instructions expressed in words, codes, schemes, or any other form, including a machine readable medium, capable of causing a computer to perform a particular task or achieve a particular result," when read with section 2(o) of the Copyright Act 1957, which defines "literary works" as "computer programmes, tables, and compilations, including computer databases," protects software or a computer database.

Whenever a software application is filed in the copyright office for registration, the applicant shows the copy of the source code and the object code, which in a way is the expression and art of the applicant.

Therefore, it can be concluded that Copyright law can be understood to apply on Metaverse aspects and activities conducted in this digital world once it is launched in India and legal framework is decided to be implemented on this platform. As per the law, Copyright exists with the IP Creator who has created that particular work as stated under Section 17 of the Copyright Act of 1957. The coders can be known as the IP creator, and they will have to pay royalties for other IP used in an avatar, such as likeness of a person, clothes, distinctive features and etc.

<u>CONCLUSION</u>

The technological breakthroughs required for a true metaverse will be enormous – the metaverse would require hundreds of thousands, if not millions, of digital avatars interacting with one another. To give this a scale, popular video games can currently only handle up to 150 people in a single virtual environment.

While the emergence of a true metaverse is no longer a "if," but rather a "when", owing to the different countries, the manner in which the metaverse will evolve over time is unclear. In a dystopian future, some predict that a single business will be able to build and own the metaverse. In the IP perspective, this seems like a positive start for the IP owners in the metaverse realm, and as time passes, more clarity will be provided owing to the glaring IP issues that will crop up and owners, lawyers interested in the metaverse would want to continue to keep an eye on these developments closely.

Author's Biography

My name is Ashish Gupta and I have done my B.A.LLB from National Law Institute University, Bhopal whereas my Post graduation (LL.M) under the specialization of Intellectual Property Rights has been from Gujarat National Law University, Gandhinagar. Currently, I am working as a Freelancer Blogger and interested in exploring various areas of Intellectual Property Rights through the medium of blogging.

CHAPTER TEN

REMEDIES IN TRADEMARK LAW – ORDERS AND INJUNCTIONS

Author: Ashish Gupta, LL.M(IPR) from Gujarat National Law University, Gandhinagar

Introduction

Litigation in India is a form of dispute resolution mechanism that is popular. For a litigation proceeding to end, the institutions approached i.e.,

Court of law shall either dispose off the matter or pronounce a judgement on it, if the dispute is not withdrawn by the parties themselves. Similarly, in Trademark litigation proceedings, when the Court of law pronounces a judgement, it is given via different and various forms.

Remedies

The following are some of the actions that can be done to protect trade marks in India, including actions against infringement and passing off:

1. Cease and Desist notice, or
2. Civil Action, or
3. Criminal Proceedings, or
4. Border Measure.

This study shall analyze the means to sought a Trademark dispute. The courts in India, have adopted a certain practice which includes different set of actions. Emphasis on the different orders and injunctions is provided as part of Civil Action, where major Trademark proceedings head to.

Civil Action

Civil remedies can be pursued by bringing a complaint in a competent court for either infringement or passing off or both of these. In addition, the following civil reliefs are made available to a victim:

Interlocutory/Temporary/Ad-interim Injunction

This injunction prevents a party to a lawsuit from taking any action until the case is resolved. It is a discretionary remedy that is only granted if the plaintiff can show a prima facie case that the comparative inconvenience to the parties is in their favor, and that if a temporary redressal or in this case an injunction is not granted, they will suffer irrevocable harm.

Mareva Injunction

Their assets are frozen as a result of the Mareva injunction. Neither is granted lightly, and it is critical to have all of the necessary supporting documents in order before approaching the court.

It's a legal term for injunctions that prevent the Defendant from transferring any asset or property from the jurisdiction or dealing with or disposing of them in such a way that makes the Plaintiff's decree granted a simple brutum fulmen (valueless).

In India, a Mareva injunction can be obtained under the CPC's Order 38 Rule 5 and 6 or Order 39 Rule 1. The criteria that a Plaintiff must prove in order to obtain a Mareva order are similar to those required for an interim injunction - a prima facie case, balance of convenience, and irrevocable harm.

Elements

1. There must be a valid cause of action, and the Plaintiff must make a good arguable case when the order is to be granted.
2. Defendant shall have assets located within the Court's territorial jurisdiction.
3. Balance of convenience should slightly favour granting the injunction to the Plaintiff.
4. The Plaintiff should be able to show that the Defendant is dishonest in addition to the substantial risk of wealth dissipation existing.
5. No time has passed since the injunction was requested.

Anton Pillar Orders

The Anton Piller order, which is a type of discovery preservation given on an ex parte application, is a very powerful weapon in the plaintiff's arsenal. It can include an injunction to permission for plaintiff's authorized official to enter the premises or the establishment of the defendant for the purpose of inspecting documents and collect originals, permission to remove the alleged wrongful goods and even destruction of the said wrongful goods, if need be, to destroy defendant's establishment and image earned and gained through illegal means, and an injunction prohibiting defendants from revealing the content of the injunction to third parties

It is similar to a search warrant, but this order permits the search of the asset or property without the consent of the defendant.

John Doe Orders

The plaintiffs, with the help of court-appointed local commissioners, have virtually unrestricted powers to raid any property where infringement may take place under John Doe orders, which translates to virtually absolute powers available to the plaintiffs, with the help of local commissioners or officers who are permitted to raid any property where activities like any sort of infringement takes place.

Permanent/Perpetual Injunction

This injunction is a court order requiring a party, person (living) or entity to abstain from doing specific things indefinitely or execute particular measures indefinitely.

Damages or Accounts of Profits

Damages or accounting of profits are the Plaintiff's two mutually exclusive remedies. The rightful owner is awarded damages to compensate for the losses he or she has suffered as a result of the infringer's actions. This remedy is proving to be an equitable remedy that demands the infringer to simply return the real amounts of earnings he made as a result of the infringing acts to the rightful owner of the IP.

Delivery-up and Destruction

The infringing subject is delivered to the rightful owner under this remedy or it is destroyed.

Cease And Desist Notice

- If a person or a company infringes on a trademark, copyrighted work, patent, or industrial design, the owner can issue a cease-and-desist notice to the infringing party, informing them of the intellectual property and related rights.
- This warning is delivered before a lawsuit against the infringing party is filed. In a C&D, the trademark owner requests that the infringer voluntarily stop from or cease infringing on the trademark owner's rights within the specified time period. If the infringer continues to infringe on the IP, the trademark owner may pursue legal action to enforce their rights.
- During legal procedures against the infringing party, a well-drafted notification serves as prima facie evidence.
- It aids the trademark owner in determining the infringing party's malicious intent in incorrectly applying the known trademark or any other IP to their goods and services.

The advantages are as follows:

a. It establishes the owner's rights in their IP;

b. It establishes the owner's attempt to reach an amicable resolution in the matter by informing the infringing party of the offensive activity; and

c. It allows the influencing party to end their influencing operations in connection to the IP within the time frame specified.

d. Rather than initiating an infringement litigation, it is a much more cost-effective and efficient way to deal with IP infringement.

Criminal Proceedings

The Trade Marks Act of 1999 is the sole statute in India that governs the law of trademarks. Infringing any registered trademark, producing falsified trademarks, applying false trade descriptions, applying false indications of origin country, and so on are all covered by the aforementioned statute. Infringement of trademark in the food and medicine industries is stated as a punishable offence. Punishments for criminal proceedings include a maximum penalty of three years in prison with or without a fine which shall vary from offence to offence, but the term mentioned is the maximum time period.

Border Measures

Custom Officers are empowered to enforce the Intellectual Property Rights over imported goods under the IPR (Imported Goods) Enforcement Rules in the year 2007. The rules outline a step-by-step process for a right holder to register their Intellectual Property Right. The Indian Customs Act, 1962 also gives the Central Government the authority to prohibit the importation or exportation of goods that have been labelled with a fake trademark or trade description.

Author's Biography

My name is Ashish Gupta and I have done my B.A.LLB from National Law Institute University, Bhopal whereas my Post graduation (LL.M) under the specialization of Intellectual Property Rights has been from Gujarat National Law University, Gandhinagar. Currently, I am working as a Freelancer Blogger and interested in exploring various areas of Intellectual Property Rights through the medium of blogging.

CHAPTER ELEVEN

SCOPE OF HIGHCOURT UNDER DESIGN ACT 2000 CASE ANALYSIS OF M/S MOLD TEK PACKING LTD.V. S.D.CONTAINERS

Author: Ashish Gupta, LL.M(IPR) from Gujarat National Law University, Gandhinagar

This dispute is not a classic registered design dispute, but also a dispute regarding the jurisdiction. Whether the High Court in M.P. has the jurisdiction or the High Court in West Bengal. The Hon'ble Supreme Court has been approached via a Special Leave Petition (SLP) under Article 136 of the Constitution.

Facts

Initially, M/S Mold Tek filed a suit for declaration to obtain a permanent injunction against S. D. Containers from using a design which had been duly registered under the Design Act in the Commercial District court which was used in some of the containers and lids they manufacture. However, on the contrary, the contention from the Defendants/Appellants has been that said designs could not have been registered under Section 4(2) of the Design Act on the grounds that they are not novel nor original, and hence, their registration should be revoked or cancelled to be set in accordance of Section 19 of the Design Act. Section 4 states about 'prohibition of registration of certain designs' and Section 19 states about Cancellation of registration, which has been sought after by the Respondents.

In addition to this, the appellants filed another application seeking to transfer these proceedings to the MP High Court, Indore Bench. This application had been made under Section 22(4) of the act read with Section 19 (2). The further developments took an unexpected turn as the District Judge transferred these applications to the Calcutta High Court. Respondents appealed in the High Court of MP, when the Hon'ble court set aside that order of transfer of the case under Section 22(4) of the Design Act, 2000. Hon'ble Supreme Court decided to intervene and decide and interpret the jurisdiction issues arising out of this dispute between the courts under Design Act and the Commercial Courts Act.

Issue

Whether M.P. High Court or W.B. High Court have the jurisdiction to hear the matter in question?

Rule

Section 4 of the Design Act, 2000 - Prohibition of registration of certain designs

Section 19 of the Design Act, 2000- Cancellation of registration

Section 21 of the Commercial Courts Act, 2015 - Transfer of pending cases

Decision

The Apex Court stated that the suit should be transferred to MP High Court, Indore Bench since cause of action had arisen in that state.

<u>Analysis</u>

The Hon'ble Supreme Court has been approached through an appeal in this particular case and has analysed the relationship of the provisions of the Commercial Courts Act and the Design Act. In a situation like this where one party alleged a use of a registered design by another party or where cancellation of a design is sought by the Respondents, there are two options available to the complainant. Those options are:

Approach Controller under Section 19 of the Design Act, 2000

The text of this provision states that "An appeal shall lie from any order of the Controller under this section to the High Court". This provision also enables any aggrieved party to approach the controller for cancellation of a registered design.

Approach High Court under Section 22 (4) of the Design Act, 2000

This provision states about 'Piracy of registered design', and "where any ground on which the registration of a design may be cancelled under section 19 has been availed of as a ground of defence under sub-section (3) in any suit or other proceeding for relief under sub-section (2), the suit or such other proceeding shall be transferred by the court, in which the suit or such other proceeding is pending, to the High Court for decision."

<u>**Where did the aspect of Commercial Courts Act come from?**</u>

The inclusion of Commercial Courts Act comes from the interpretation by the Apex Court, scrutinizing the Section 21 of the act, which states that the Commercial Courts Act shall have a precedence over cases in case of conflict with any existing law/statute, which has been the case in the present scenario with jurisdiction disputes as to whether MP High Court or West Bengal High Court.

The crucial aspect analysed by the court was that the act "gives an overriding effect, only if the provisions of the Act have anything inconsistent with any other law for the time being in force." This is interpreted according to the literal interpretation. Hence, the Hon'ble Apex court concluded that the Commercial Courts Act cannot possibly put a stop to the transfer of proceedings to the High Court as there are no inconsistencies relating to the Design act and the stipulated law, meaning that Commercial Courts act does not apply.

<u>**Jurisdiction Of The High Court**</u>

The Apex court has stated about the options for the cancellation of registration i.e., with the Controller, and which can be appealed before the High Court. The MP High Court had relied on the case of M/S Godrej Sara Lee Limited vs Reckitt Benckiser Australia (CIVIL APPEAL NOS. 996-997/2010), wherein a plea for cancellation of a design had been made in accordance with Section 19, and the decision was that High Court had jurisdiction in case of appeal only. Thus, it dealt with Section 19(2), while the present suit deals with action under Section 22(4). The court has stated that Sections 19(2) and 22(4) are independent provisions, and hence, question of whether 'independent' means that the two provisions can operate simultaneously.

The Commercial Court, Indore had initially transferred the present suit to West Bengal High Court, as the designs were registered in that state. The court referring to the Godrej Sara Lee case held that jurisdiction lies within the High court where the 'cause of action' arises. Since the suit had been filed in Indore and no part of the cause of action had arisen in Kolkata, the Supreme Court transferred the suit to MP High Court, Indore Bench.

The cited Godrej Sara Lee case consists of observations of a cancellation action under Section 19. Hence, the Supreme court had stated one of the cause of actions was the cancellation of registration itself, that took place in Kolkata, rendering the jurisdiction with the Calcutta High Court applicable.

But the key point to be noted is that in case of a cancellation action under Section 19, the jurisdiction lies with the High Court where the cancellation action has been taken. And in case of a counter-claim in an infringement suit, the cause of action arises where the suit has been initially filed by the Plaintiff, which was Indore, and in this present case a counter claim has indeed been filed.

In cases like these, the Hon'ble Supreme Court has often applied the 'prima facie tenable' test which is often put to use "to further the cause of justice by elimination of false, frivolous and untenable claims of invalidity that may be raised in the suit". A test of this nature helps perform a preliminary assessment which helps avoid wasting of time. This test can be applied in the present situation for assessing design infringement disputes before transferring it to the High Court under Section 22(4). The Supreme Court's decision of concluding that the jurisdiction exists with the court of original appellate jurisdiction as well as counter-claim jurisdiction in the present case seems to be sound in law and a step in the right direction.

<u>**Conclusion**</u>

This judgment by the Supreme Court has brought clarity to the interpretation of the complex provisions such as Sections 19, 22 of the Design Act, and Section 21 of the Commercial Courts Act. The court relied on different high court judgements in the deciding the commercial court jurisdiction issue. If MP High Court's decision had not been petitioned for appeal and the Supreme Court had not adjudicated on it, the decision would have created conflicting precedents. Hopefully, in the future a similar provision could be added in the Designs Act, 2000 that clears out the ambiguity regarding the appellate jurisdiction to approach a High Court.

Author's Biography

My name is Ashish Gupta and I have done my B.A.LLB from National Law Institute University, Bhopal whereas my Post graduation (LL.M) under the specialization of Intellectual Property Rights has been from Gujarat National Law University, Gandhinagar. Currently, I am working as a Freelancer Blogger and interested in exploring various areas of Intellectual Property Rights through the medium of blogging.

CHAPTER TWELVE

IS BEING A TRANSGENDER A SIN?

Author: Harshita Dixit, II Year of B.B.A.,LL.B from Maharaja Agrasen Institute of Management Studies.

Linda Thompson a famous American songwriter once said "Being a transgender, being tall, being gay, white or black, male or female, is another part of humans which makes us unique and something over we have no control. We are who we are in the deepest recesses of our mind, hearts, and identities."

Transgender is a term which is used to describe a person whose gender identity or gender expression differs from their biological sex. A transperson's struggle to survive starts from childhood. Most are abandoned by their families, denied education. In order to provide social, economic and educational empowerment, the supreme court judgement ruled out in NALSA v. INDIA that transgender people should be recognised as a third gender enjoying all their fundamental rights, while also being entitled to specific benefits like purchasing, renting properties, holding public offices.

Subsequently, in order to protect the rights of transgender, 20th November is celebrated as transgender Remembrance Day. It was first observed in 1999 by a transgender advocate Gwendolyn Ann smith to honour the memory of Rita haster, a transgender who was stabbed 20 times in her own apartment.

But little we know about the heinous crimes they go through. The number of real incidents of heinous crimes against transgender is 10 or 11 times higher than the ones reported with the police. The difference in numbers is largely because of the little legal sanction to act on rapes and sexual violence. In addition to that, the provision for punishment for serious crimes committed against transgender people is substantially less severe than for the same crimes committed towards other communities like the penalty for rape of a transgender is merely just six months to two years. Second, and more concerning is the apparent, contempt, prejudice and disdain against their community.

For instance, on 15th January 2019, Alka a 23-years-old transwoman left her house to visit the tattapni festival in Chhattisgarh, did she realize that while visiting she would meet two people and amongst them would be an alleged rapist? Did she realize it would be her last day just? She was brutally murdered because she was a trans gender and not a cisgender. Another unspeakable instance happened in June 2017; a 19 years old transgender woman was gangraped by four men in pune. When she went to the hospital, the doctors were asking questions about how a transgender could possibly get raped. Even the nurses were rude. This lack of sensitivity and understandability, in most the cases, open hostility and transphobia, discourage transgender from seeking legal remedies. Every year across the world numerous transgender persons are murdered simply because of who they are. A much higher number of sexual violences goes unreported. This is the price which they pay for just simply existing.

Consequently, this leads to a scenario where begging and sex work becomes their only options to earn and survive. Being forced into sex work puts transgender at the risk of contracting sexually transmitted diseases, and takes away their agency over their bodies, along with violating their fundamental rights.

Society looks at them with pity and disgusting eyesight. Nevertheless, they have risen irrespective of all bigotry and challenges. Some of the famous and known are Padmini Prakash who scripted history by becoming the first transgender woman to anchor a local new channel in Lotus. another known yet inspiring is K Prithika Yashini who became the first transgender police officer in India. If these people can survive and try to prosper in a society which sees them as impure then isn't it our choice and responsibility to stop the societal behavioural negative norms towards them?

I dare to dream of a world where people can dress, speak and behave how they want, free from mockery, judgement and danger. This is what I want. Who's with me?

Author's Biography

I am Harshita Dixit, a second year law student pursuing BBA LLB from Maharaja Agrasen Institute of Management Studies. I am an enthusiastic writer who loves to write articles relating to socio-political issues. My professional goals have always been exploring each and every opportunity I see. Being a law aspirant, I have acquired research, analytical and communicative skills. Apart from my academics, I am a certified Bharatanatyam dancer as well as an athlete.

SECTION 188 OF THE INDIAN PENAL CODE- APPLICABILITY & RELEVANCE OF SECTION 188 IN COVID-19 SITUATION

Author: Khushi, I year of B.B.A.,LL.B from The Northcap University.

As we all are well aware our country, as well as the whole world, is suffering from the adverse situation created due to the pandemic COVID-19. In order to control the situation as well as to curb the speed or spread of COVID-19 or its various variants, various guidelines and standard of procedures have been issued by the Central as well as the State government. In order to fulfil the aforesaid guidelines, the order in this regard is being passed by the various authorities which are required to be followed in the present situation. Every citizen is required to follow and obey the orders passed by the authorities from time to time. But we can see that the aforesaid orders are not being followed in their true spirit and are being violated. Now the question comes whether by violating such order any offence has been committed or not. Section 188 of the Indian Penal Code deals with the disobedience to order duly promulgated by the public servant.

Definition of Section 188 of the Indian Penal Code

Whoever, knowing that, by an order promulgated by the public servant lawfully empowered to promulgate such order, he is directed to abstain from a certain act or to take certain order with certain property in his possession or under his management disobeys such directions, shall, if such disobedience causes or tends to cause obstruction, annoyance or injury, or risk of obstruction, annoyance or injury to any persons lawfully employed, be punished with simple imprisonment for a term which may extend to 1 month or with fine which may extend to Rs 200, or with both;

And if such disobedience causes or tends to cause danger to human life, health, or safety, or causes or tends to cause a riot or affray, shall be punished with imprisonment of either description for a term which may extend to six months or with fine which may extend to Rs 1000 or with both.

Every citizen of India has constitutional rights and with the rights, they are also required to obey the law of land. If any person commits any act which is in violation of the law that amounts to an offence and disobeying of any order duly promulgated by the public servant is being dealt with the aforesaid Section 188 of The Indian Penal Code.

Ingredients for the commission of an offence under Section 188 of The Indian Penal Code

1. Promulgation of an order must be in existence and it should be made by a public servant who was legally empowered to make such promulgation.

2. A direction should be there not to do certain things.

3. Offender must be aware of promulgation and the same was disobeyed by him.

4. Such disobedience has caused or tended to cause obstruction or annoyance, injury or risk of the same to a person lawfully employed or accused or tendered to cause danger to human life, health or safety or a riot or an affray.

According to the book 'The Indian Penal Code' by authors Ratanlal and Dhirajlal (19th edition), "There must be evidence that the accused had knowledge of the order with the disobedience of which he is charged. Mere proof of a general notification promulgating the order does not satisfy the requirements of the section. Mere disobedience of the order does not constitute an offence in itself, it must be shown that the disobedience has or tends to a certain consequence."

The actual problem arises which is being debated nowadays in the legal circle. The argument is that an offence under Section 188 of the Indian Penal Code is a specified offence. Procedurally, envisaged in Section 195, CrPC, and therefore unless the requirements are satisfied no action can be initiated against any individual.

Case laws

In this regard, the legal position can be understood with the following case laws.

In the case of Jeevanandham v. State, 2018 the Madras High Court held that it is mandatory to follow the procedure of Section 195 of CrPC, 1973 to prosecute an accused of an offence under Section 188 of IPC otherwise such action would be rendered as void ab initio. There must be a complaint by the public servant whose lawful order has not been complied with. The power of police officers is limited to preventive action and immediately he has to inform the concerned public servant to enable him to proceed with the complaint before the Court.

In the case of Jagdish and others v, the State of Haryana, 2015 the Punjab and Haryana High Court held that as per Section 195(1) of the CrPC, 1973 no FIR can be registered by the police unless there is a written complaint made by the public servant concerned and if made then the police report will be quashed for the offence under Section 188 of IPC.

Being the cognizable offence, the police have the power to take action to prevent such an offence from being committed and may arrest a person without a warrant as provided for in Section 41 of the Criminal Procedure Code. The police have the power to register an FIR and proceed to investigate such an offence and may proceed to prepare a report consequent to such investigation.

A person cannot take a defense that he has no knowledge that disobedience may cause harm. If he disobeyed the order the person is liable to be punished under this act. The actual harm or intention to harm others is not necessary for the commission of this offence. The mere fact that he disobeyed the order despite knowledge of the passing of such an order is sufficient to hold him liable for the commission of an offence. The offence under Section 188 of the Indian Penal Code is a cognizable and bailable offence. It is triable by any magistrate.

Conclusion

Recently, the Hon'ble Supreme court has quoted in its judgment that the people not wearing a mask in public spaces are violating the fundamental Right to Life of others. They may hamper the health of other people. There is a lack of will everywhere. Everybody is moving without masks in markets, malls, marriage, etc., and enhancing the fine may not suffice until there is proper implementation. In the present scenario, the administration is passing the orders to follow the COVID-19 protocols, to use masks in public places, and to maintain social distancing as well as to avoid unnecessary gatherings. If a person violates these directions in that case, it gave rise to a danger to human life, health, and safety of the public. Hence the violation of the same is an offence as provided under Section 188 of the Indian Penal Code and is punishable with simple imprisonment of 6 months or fine up to Rs 1000 or with both.

Author's Biography

I am Khushi . I am the student of BBA-LL.B 1st year 1 Semester of The Northcap University.I have written the blog on the topic "Section-188 of The Indian Penal Code- Applicability and Relevance of Section 188 in COVID-19 situation as it is a current arising topic.

CHAPTER FOURTEEN

TRACING THE EVOLUTION OF THE CONCEPT OF ORIGNALITY IN COPYRIGHT LAW:DOCTRINE OF SWEAT OF THE BROW TO DOCTRINE OF MODICUM OF CREATIVITY

<u>Author</u>: Anshika Tiwari, IV year of B.A.,LL.B(Hons.) From Hidayatullah National Law University Raipur.

ABSTRACT

Copyright is a bundle of exclusive legal rights accruing to any person who is a creator of literary, dramatic, artistic and musical works. These rights enable the originator to protect his work from unauthorised reproduction, duplication and use by others.

Section 13 of the Copyright Act of 1957 categorically states that copyright shall subsist in 'original' literary, dramatic, musical and artistic works; cinematograph films and sound recording. The aforesaid categories of works have been qualified by the word 'original' meaning thereby originality is the sine qua non of copyright protection under the act.

Originality requirement is thus an inseparable part of copyright protection and the former and latter go hand in hand.

While the act does lay down what are the kinds of original works eligible for protection, it nowhere does provide what is the quantum of originality that would suffice to obtain protection. Since the legislation remains silent on the question of how much original a work ought or ought not to be, this vital question has mostly been left to be decided by the courts throughout jurisdictions.

INTRODUCTION

Originality in the context of copyright protection is not construed in its literal sense. It does not mean something unique or unheard of. A work, in order to be original under the copyright realm need not be the first of its kind. Intellectual Property law recognises the fact that each work is bound to have some degree of influence from the earlier works of the same kind.

The only originality expected for copyright protection is some element of human endeavour or creativity. The work should not be something novel but the only thing expected of it is that it should not be a mere copy of another work. What will be the extent of this creativity was a hazy area and there still is no definite standard of originality. Different countries follow different doctrines to assess originality in a work. The two most common ones are the Doctrine of Sweat of the Brow and The Doctrine of Modicum of Creativity.

DOCTRINE OF SWEAT OF THE BROW

Stated simply, this doctrine gives due credit and protection to a creator's work as long as he as toiled over it in some or the other way. This doctrine recognises the labour both human and material put in by the author in his work irrespective of any ingenuity his work may or may not contain.

According to the sweat of the brow doctrine, simple diligence exercised in the course of creating the work is sufficient for granting copyright protection. It dispenses with the creativity requirement altogether.

Mere industrious gathering or putting together of data or facts even when such compilation lacks any imagination or judgement entitles the compiler to copyright protection under this approach. Going by this doctrine, dictionaries, encyclopedias, almanacs and gazettes are as much a subject of copyright protection as any other creative work notwithstanding the fact that they are mere compilations of pre-existing facts without any creative thought process involved.

Origin of the Doctrine

This doctrine took birth in UK in the 1900 in the famous case of Walter vs. Lane.

In this case, the oral addresses given by the then Prime Minister of UK, Earl of Rosebery, were jotted down by the reporters of The Times newspaper in the form of short notes. Later, these speeches were reproduced verbatim in the form of newspaper reports. Thereafter the respondents also published a book containing the speeches, the content of which was sourced from the newspaper reports. The proprietors of the newspapers sued the publisher John Lane for copyright violation. The litigation concerned a book published by Lane entitled "Appreciations and Addresses delivered by Lord Rosebery" in which allegedly a series of reports formerly published in The Times was copied word by word.

The question before the court in this case was whether the reporters who reproduced the speeches word to word would be qualified as authors under the Copyright Act 1842?

The Court of Appeal initially said that since the reproduction contained nothing original, it will not entail copyright protection. However the House of Lords reversed the previous decision. The House of Lords held that the reporters were authors of these speeches within meaning of Copyright Act 1842. It found that the process of creating the reports involved efforts, skill and judgement which were sufficient to make the reporters' work original. This is still the position in UK and the decision in Walter v Lane [1900] is considered as the authority for the notion of "originality" in the UK copyright law.

The doctrine of sweat of the brow protects any form of factual compilation, the only requirement being that it should not be a borrowed effort. This school of thought altogether discards creativity as a requirement for copyright protection. Thus, the doctrine holds that labour or industry per se is sufficient to make the work original and hence copyrightable. Any work which is original in the sense that it is not copied from that of another is copyrightable even though it may be just a mechanical work.

"UNIVERSITY OF LONDON PRESS LIMITED vs. UNIVERSITY TUTORIAL PRESS LIMITED"

The University of London appointed two examiners and they were entrusted with the task of setting papers for matriculation examinations. They were at liberty to choose their questions given the syllabus and the knowledge expected from students. The University of London issued a resolution to the effect that the copyright of all papers set by the examiners employed by them shall vest with the university itself. The University entered into an agreement with the University of London Press Limited whereby the copyright and all rights to publish the matriculation examination papers were assigned to the latter in lieu of a consideration. Later, a publication was made by the University Tutorial Press Limited which included sixteen out of forty-two matriculation papers. The papers were not copied from the publication of the University of London Press Limited, but were taken from copies of the examination papers supplied by students. In addition to the question papers, the publication also contained answers to those questions and it criticised the manner in which the questions were framed. The plaintiff, University of London Press, brought a suit against University Tutorial Press for copyright infringement.

The question before the court was whether the question papers were an 'original literary work' within the meaning of the act?

The stand of the plaintiff was that the term "literary work" as used in the Act covered a broad ambit and included all works expressed in print or writing, irrespective of whether the quality or style is high and includes maps, charts, plans, tables, and compilations. Therefore the examination papers will also fall under the category of "literary work".

The defendant, on the contrary contended that the questions were of a common category and there was nothing unique or distinct enough to attract copyright protection.

The Court held that,

"Copyright Act does not require that expression be in an original or novel form; the only condition is that it should originate from the author". The plaintiffs had already proved to the satisfaction of the court that they had thought out the questions themselves. "The question papers are original within the meaning of copyright laws as they originated from the authors." The court held that the plaintiff's claim for copyright cannot be dismissed merely because similar questions have been asked by other examiners as well.

Thus, the court made it clear that originality cannot be equated with novelty.

"LADBROKE vs. WILLIAM HILL"

This case arose in Britain in the early sixties and the dispute was concerned with infringement of copyright vested in the football betting coupons issued by the respondents, William Hill Football Ltd. The respondents had been using the coupons since the early 1950s. Subsequently, in 1969, the appellants decided to enter the field and began sending out coupons substantially similar to those of the respondents.

The respondents brought a copyright claim against the appellants, Ladbroke (Football) Ltd. Ladbroke admitted the fact that they had copied the material of William Hill but said that they were mere compilations and had no protection on them.

The House of Lords ruled in favour of William Hill and held that the betting coupons were "original" if not artistic compilations and were subject to copyright protection.

Rationale

In delivering their judgment, the Lords emphasised the amount of work, money and ingenuity or uniqueness that the plaintiff's work bore of which the defendants carried out a substantial copying. The decision cemented the centrality of the requirement of "labour, skill and/or judgment" to any finding of originality.

"BURLINGTON HOME SHOPPING PVT LTD vs. RAJNISH CHIBBER"

The plaintiff in this case was in the business of direct mail marketing under which his company used to offer consumer merchandise by publishing catalogues in newspapers/magazines which were posted to a select list of clients who used to then place orders by email. For the purpose of the business, the plaintiff had compiled a customer database or clientele by investing substantial amount of money and efforts.

The defendant used to work with the plaintiff's company but had no role in the compilation business. After severing ties with the plaintiff company, he started his own business in the same field as a competitor of the plaintiffs. He caught hold of the customer database of the plaintiffs and used the same to contact the clients of the former and establishing business relations with the plaintiff's customers.

The plaintiff contended that the defendants have infringed their copyright in the database. The question here was whether a compilation of mailing addresses of customers amounted to original literary work and whether any copyright subsisted in such a work. The court inter alia relied upon the judgments of the William Hill case and that of Govindan vs Gopalakrishna and answered the question in the affirmative.

It held,

"Compilation of addresses developed by any one by devoting time, money labour and skill though the sources may be commonly situated amounts to a 'literary work' wherein the author has a copyright." "The determining factor in finding whether another person's copyright has been infringed is to see whether the impugned work is a slavish imitation and copy of another person's work or it bears the impress of the author's own labours and exertions."

DOCTRINE OF MODICUM OF CREATIVITY

There has been a paradigm shift in the standard of originality and there has been an inclination to move towards a more wholesome, inclusive and logical approach which does not merely reward diligence but also looks for traces of intellect, creative endeavour and judgement in the work.

This doctrine stipulates that, in addition to being an independent creation, the work must also exhibit a modicum of creativity. Labour or toil by the author does not guarantee artistic merit and therefore it is necessary to look beyond the efforts and see if the work has any traces of creativity or not. The threshold of creativity required is not too high but only a minimum amount of creative effort in the work is sufficient.

The Supreme Court of USA straightaway rejected the doctrine of Sweat of the Brow in the case of Feist Publications, Inc. v. Rural telephone Service Co.

Rural Telephone Service Company was in the service of providing telephone services. A local law required all telephone service providers to issue an up to date telephone directory on a yearly basis. Using the available data Rural Telephone Co. published its directory. Feist Publications Inc. was a publishing company whose directories covered a wide geography and included 11 different telephone service areas. Both the companies used to earn revenue from yellow page advertising. Feist did not have an independent access to any subscriber information and thus it used to approach telephone companies in its area for getting listings. Rural Telephone Co refused to license its listings to Feist after which the latter used them without permission. Feist then hired personnel to investigate and verify the data. Therefore Feist's listing had more information than those of Rural's. Since some listings of Feist were identical to that of Rural Telephone Co, the latter brought an action against Feist for violation of copyright in its compilations. The question was whether a compilation akin to a telephone directory is a subject to copyright protection.

The Court held that facts per se are not copyrightable but compilations of facts are. This was due to the fact that compilations demonstrated a unique way of representing facts, used different ways of arranging them. They possessed a minimal degree of creativity and were hence copyrightable. The Court held that Rural's directory failed to meet the required minimum benchmark of creativity as it was just a compilation of data. A work, in order to be protected must possess something more than a de minimis quantum of creativity which Rural's work fell short of.

Arranging telephone numbers and basic subscriber information in alphabetical order was nothing novel and was a common practice in telephone directories. Copyright rewards creativity and not effort and since Rural's work itself lacked originality, there was no way Feist's work could be said to be infringing it. Hence, their case against Feist was dismissed.

WHAT IS THE INDIAN SCENARIO?

In India, the doctrine of Brow sweat was followed for a considerably long period of time. However, it was in the case of Eastern Book Company vs. D.B. Modak that the court discarded it and moved to the modicum of creativity standard as followed in the US.

The question before the court in this case was,

What is the standard of originality required in a derivative work to render it fit for copyright protection?

The appellant (s) EBC and Eastern Publishers Pvt Ltd were in the business of publishing law books. They published a law report by the name of SCC which contained all the supreme court cases procured from the apex court's register.

The judgements were edited to make them user oriented and for this fonts and paragraph formatting were changed and head notes and foot notes inserted.

The respondents created a software and copy pasted the entire report of the plaintiffs on a CD ROM. In particular, EBC alleged that the defendants' have copied EBC's sequencing, selection and arrangement of the cases along with the entire text of the edited judgements verbatim.

The Court held, "The derivative work produced by the author must have some distinguishable features and flavour to raw text of the judgments delivered by the court". The judgements of the courts are in public domain therefore free to be used by anyone so there cannot be any copyright over them. However, the appellants had expended considerable skill and intellect in editing the judgements. The way the judgments are presented in the reports; includes footnoting, editorial notes, cross-referencing, selection, sequencing, and arrangement of the judgments, making it the original work of art in itself; entirely different from the actual raw data collected from the register of the supreme court. This by no means is merely a mechanical process, but also a skilful use of personal brain, the court said

The rationale behind the verdict was that any derivative work should substantially differ from the original work and must add some value to it. This decision was a path breaking judgement in the course of jurisprudential development of copyright law in India.

The court, instead of relying on any one doctrine solely, found a middle ground and attempted to harmoniously reconcile the persistent conflict between the doctrine of sweat of the brow and modicum of creativity.

By the judgement the court made it clear that the standard of originality is not so steep that the work needs to be extremely innovative or unconventional but at the same time it is also not so low that mere application of labour and capital would render it copyrightable. What is required is 'Exercise of one's skill and judgement' in the work.

<u>CONCLUSION AND SUGGESTION</u>

The aim of copyright law is to maintain an equilibrium between granting copyright protection as a form of incentive for the author and at the same time restricting overprotection which may result in monopolisation of a an author over a particular work/genre of work. For this very reason the cardinal principle followed is that only expression is copyrightable and not the idea itself. Copyright subsists over an original expression and originality is the sine qua non of copyright protection. Law has been practical enough to hold that this originality does not mean novelty or uniqueness; it only means that the work should originate from the author and not just be an imitation of previous works. The doctrine of sweat of the brow believes that mere industry or labour is sufficient to grant protection. While this is still the norm in most common law countries, including UK, the United States transitioned to the modicum of creativity approach which gives primacy to some amount of creative effort. This approach is more plausible and logical as in my opinion it fulfils better the underlying motive behind copyright law. Every work claiming copyright protection must bear an imprint of the author's personality, must be substantially different from what is already available.

The threshold of creativity cannot be too high as it will lead to majority of works falling outside copyright purview and the same time it cannot be so low so as to offer protection to every copied work having just trivial modifications. The balance between the two approaches is the key so that every genuine effort is rewarded and at the same time no one can enjoy protection riding upon the work of another.

<u>Author's Biography</u>

A penultimate year student at Hidayatullah National Law University with keen interest in subjects of Constitutional Law and Intellectual Property Rights inter alia.

CHAPTER FIFTEEN

HAS DISCREPANCIES IN E-COMMERCE TRANSACTION SECURITY LED TO FRAUD?

Author: Deepanjali K.S, IV Year of B.Com, LL.B. from Ramaiah College of Law.

ABSTRACT

Technology, these days have become the part and parcel of a human's life. It would not be wrong to say that without these advancements it will, become difficult to conduct day-to-day living. If we could recall the usage of the internet in India, which was roughly started in the year 1995. For over a decade the internet was merely for browsing. But these days the internet has developed to such an extent that, all the activities can be done in one clickbait, for example, order of groceries. The fact that these high-end facilities have their disadvantages. The researcher in this particular paper has tried the highlight, how people using the technology associated with payment of money, with the help of electronic devices like mobile or computer, have been fraudulently robbed. However, this paper does not neglect the importance of such platforms, for various reasons like, how they contribute to the economy or the easy access to resources. For instance, E-commerce or E-trade in the global market has drastically increased during a pandemic, global retail trade from 19% in 2019 to 17% in 2020. It would not be wrong to say that pandemic has accelerated digital transformation. However, this acceleration was also backed by online frauds, which made the pandemic an academic. With the increased usage of technology and emerging threats with it. It becomes very important to regulate the system of protection of online frauds. This article only focuses on the various types of frauds and how RBI and central have tried to protect people from fraudsters.

KEYWORDS: E-transaction, internet, customers, technology, frauds, privacy, scams, digital payment, payment channels.

<u>INTRODUCTION</u>

The term transaction is usually used to describe the transfer of money or goods between persons or a business. For an activity to be termed as a transaction it has to meet two ends, i.e., starting point to the endpoint, such a transaction will have all the contractual obligations. E-transactions, e-commerce, or e-wallets are the financial terms involving the transfer of money or goods which in most cases does not involve the physical presence of the two parties entering the contract of transfer, therefore they can be put into one broad category called electronic, which is popularly connoted with letter 'e', it is very clear by know transactions that are done electronically or online is called E- transactions. But when the word E-transaction is used by IT operations, fraud, and channel managers, it takes on a more complex meaning. In application performance monitoring (APM) terms, drilling deeper into what appears to be a seamless transaction on the surface usually reveals a number of messages and distinct operations being correlated and performed beneath it. The number of related interactions making up the transaction is dependent on the number of applications and services actually "touched" along the transaction's end-to-end path. However, there is a certain major contribution of e-commerce is that there is immense growth in the GDP graph. The digital economy has grown substantially, as there is an increased rate of job creation, improved productivity, enhanced customer choice, etc, India has witnessed consistent growth in recent years and the government has been investing in many e- transactional applications such as BHIM, Digidhan Abhiyaan, Ebiz and many more, which in turn would facilitate in easy transactions of digital money and optimistic utility of internet. India ranks at 2nd largest market operating online marketing. The motive is to develop a safe bridge between stakeholders of commercial activities and the end consumers with secured Indian cyberspace. Banks and financial institutions are moving towards setting up their own setups to mitigate the transfer of funds on digital platforms. And definitely the era of globalization that has helped business activities setup in faster and more manageable form for effective commercial transaction.

COMPLEXITY ASSOCIATED WITH E-TRANSACTIONS

The fact that e-transfers have been encountered has an effective way to conduct day-to-day business, these technologies have certain issues and disputes associated with them such as contractual and non-contractual, privacy, etc. An evolved business principle of conducting business at one click bite has its own distinct and unique legal concerns which are very different from traditional business models, for example, issues concerning privacy, data security breach, and many more. Privacy concerns have been majorly discussed, since large corporations yield their customer's valuable confidential information such as credit and debit card numbers, bank account details, it is essential for the corporations to initiate strict data and cyber-crime protection regulations. Generally, e-transfers have been introduced for at most convince, which comes certain complexities associated with it majority would be in relation to cybercrimes. It is also called has computer crime because doing online transactions using computers is used as an instrument for executing illegal tasks such as committing frauds, trafficking in intellectual property, stealing identities, or privacy being violated.

There are also certain issues related to certain technical integration faced which has led consumers to not opt for these advanced services, for example, online payment systems run the proprietary gamut across hardware and software platforms. Credit card-affiliated payment processors, while more secure, can be expensive for online retailers. Added to the expense is the lack of interface between processing systems—it may be difficult or impossible for a PSP to link with other systems, resulting in processing and payment delays, lost transactions, and expensive fees. The factors associated with cyber-crime might be inadequate rules and regulations, poverty, easy accessibility of the internet, etc. which would impact on decline in financial growth, long-lasting effect on customer's personal information, and impacts on productivity and definitely change in customer behavior.

VARIOUS TYPES OF FRAUDS IN E-COMMERCE TRANSFERS

E- Transfer being the most advanced form of money transfer, allows the exchange of digital money in a few seconds. It comes with a very real and risky side effect that being the threat of loss of money online frauds. Once a person is a victim of such fraud it would put him at a vulnerable point where it would be difficult to reach out to the bank, for instant recovery of loss. Hence it is very essential for the user to be careful while using such platforms and to understand the legitimacy of the transaction in which he is getting involved. For the outline few different types of E-transfer frauds, the research paper has tried to explain, however it is not an exhaustive list.

• Authorized Push Payment Fraud:

Such a fraud occurs when a person is tricked into transferring money to a bank account that is controlled by a criminal. A customer believes that the person to whom he is transferring the amount is legitimate. For example, a fraudster could claim that he is the representative of the respective bank and ask for their details and transfer money to an account controlled by them. There are some serious kinds of fraud, which have demonized customers to use online platforms. Some of them are purchase scams, impersonation scams, malicious misdirection, investment scams, romance scams, and many more. The main reason why the fraudsters opt for AAP is the easy movement of money. However, it is might be combatted by the banks by stricter vigilance, they have involved in understanding the behavior of the transactions, also developing a strong controlled environment and protection of customer swindlers. It was also necessary to end fraud stigma among the customers.

• Account Takeover Fraud:

In this case, the fraudster uses to get access to someone else credentials and then fraudulently transfers money into their account. Information's like email addresses, phone numbers, or other personally identifiable information can be used to gain wrong access into someone's bank account. For instance, there are constant awareness messages that are created by the official to not share any kind of personal information like aadhar card number which is directly linked to the bank accounts. Organizations are also required to look into the typical engagement of a customer with the platform and also highlight the suspicious patterns.

• Money Mule Fraud:

It occurs when a person acts as a middleman between the fraudster and the person who is going to be deceived. Money mules have three main key types. Firstly, when the person is tricked into a romantic or job opportunity scheme. Secondly, here mule ignores all the warnings from the bank and continues to follow the instructions of the fraudster. Finally, there are certain kinds of individuals who are already aware of their connections to a criminal scheme, they help the fraudster to create accounts in legitimate banks for easy transfer of money. Organizations can control such events, by reviewing a wide range of information and building holistic views on mule profiles.

This isn't an exhaustive list of kinds of frauds there are certain other frauds like phishing, payroll scheme frauds, and many more. This paper has mainly focused on the most common frauds, to avoid any fraud being aware is very important.

SECURED PAYMENT SYSTEM REGULARED BY RBI

The big deterrent for the adaptation of digital payment is Cyber Crimes. There is a very thin line between secured and easy to use, it is very important to see the enforcement of the rule for secured payments and it is also essential to make such payment system cumbersome to use. Digital payment has boosted during the pandemic, the RBI has hiked the upper limit of the RTGS transaction. With which the RBI has also taken initiatives to pursue a uniform security framework for digital payment channels in the country via a proposal to Digital Payment Security Control Directions. RBI has also issued several circulars and guidelines in relation to security and risk mitigation measures for securing electronic/ digital payment systems. If someone has fraudulently withdrawn money from your bank account, inform your bank immediately. When you notify the bank, remember to take acknowledgment from your bank. The bank has to resolve your complaint within 90 days from the date of receipt. RBI's guidelines on Costumers liability in unauthorized electronic banking transfer. If the transaction has happened because of your negligence, that is, because of your sharing your password, PIN, OTP, etc., you will have to bear the loss till you report it to your bank. If the fraudulent transactions continue even after you have informed the bank, your bank will have to reimburse those amounts. If you delay the reporting, your loss will increase and it will be decided based on the RBI guidelines and the policy approved by your bank's board. The central government has also launched a cyber-crime reporting portal. The government is associated with spreading awareness about cyber-crimes alter, training, and developing of law enforcement personnel/ prosecutors/judicial forensics facilities, etc. "FCORD-FICN Coordinated Agency has been designated as Central Nodal Agency for the purpose enforcement of cyber-crime laws and for active reporting of the ADGP/IGP crime in each State/UT's.

<u>CONCLUSION</u>

Consumers in India are highly concerned about increased digital payment frauds, 60% of respondents would call their banks to block their accounts or visit the bank branch to file a written complaint in the event of fraud. Only a few report fraud activities to police or a cybercrime unit. Fake UPI payment links that ask for money transfer via text or email. A fraudster has duped users with payment requests citing donation to NGOs, contributing to PM-CARE FUND are some of the new forms of scams that has increased during the pandemic. On a positive note, there is active utilization of the platforms. The authorities and the government has continues to promote them to maintain at most safety for effective usage. Covid-19 has been a major catalyst for the growth and adaptation of digital payment in India. There was also a significant increase in online fraud cases during the pandemic. According to a study by a UK-based market research firm YouGov and NASDAQ-listed ACI Worldwide. Nearly one-third of the consumers (31%) have been a recent victim of a card or digital payment fraud or know someone among their immediate family or friends who has. Among them, 17 percent of those frauds have been within the last month. Hence it is always advised that it is very important to be aware of the online payment system, before initiating any transfer do recheck it twice. Intimation or reporting such fraud activities is also very important

CHAPTER SIXTEEN

OFFICE OF VICE PRESIDENT AND HIS POSITION IN COUNCIL OF STATES

Author: Maranganty Sreelakshmi, II Year of B.A.,LL.B from Vivekananda Institute of Professional Studies.

Introduction

The position of a Vice President in a nation is noticeable. His position is next to best in a country and he holds second highest office in the country. Part V of the Constitution of India under Chapter 1 talks about Vice President of India. Articles 63-73, which deal with the qualifications, election, and dismissal of the Vice President of India, describe everything about the Vice President. Article 63 of the Constitution Of India states " There shall be a Vice President of India".

Election of Vice President

Section 2(h) of the Presidential and Vice - Presidential Elections Act provides the definition of Vice President Election. It means an election to fill the office of the Vice President of India. Article 66 of the Indian Constitution highlight the election and eligibility criteria of the Vice President of India.

1. The Vice President shall be elected by a secret ballot by members of an electoral college comprising of members of both houses of Parliament, in accordance with the proportional representation system, using a single transferrable vote.

2. The Vice President may not be a member of either House of Parliament or a House of the Legislature of any State, and if a member of either House of Parliament or a House of the Legislature of any State is elected

Vice President, he is deemed to have vacated his seat in that House on the date he takes office as Vice President.

3. No person shall be eligible for the position of Vice President unless he is:

a) an Indian citizen;

b) Has reached the age of 35 years old ;

c) and is eligible to serve on the Council of States as a member.

4. A person is ineligible for election as Vice President if he occupies a profit-making position with the Government of India, the Government of any State, or any local or other authority under the control of any of the aforementioned Governments.

Thus, when election of Vice president takes place, no direct election is held. The designated candidate is indirectly elected by an Electoral college. However, there is difference between the college electing for the President and the Vice president. For Vice President, both nominated and elected members of both the Houses of the Parliament take part whereas for President only the elected members are eligible to elect. His elections are proportional representation. Further this article describes about the qualifications of the Vice president. It is clearly stated in the Constitution that Vice President cannot hold any office of profit under Government or outside locally. The State has no role in these elections.

<u>Term of Office of Vice President</u>

Article 67 of Constitution of India specifies about the term of office of Vice President of India.

The Vice President shall continue to be in office for a term of five years from the date on which he enters upon his office:

Provided that –

(a) A Vice President may resign his office by writing to the President;

(b) A Vice President may be removed from office by a resolution of the Council of States passed by a majority of all the then members of the Council and agreed to by the House of the People; but no resolution for the purpose of this clause shall be moved unless at least fourteen days' notice of the intention to move the resolution has been given;

(c) A Vice President shall continue to hold the office until his successor takes office, regardless of the expiration of his term.

This Article provides that the Vice President holds the office for 5 years but he can resign before the time by giving his resignation to the President. It also provides for other circumstances when there is vacancy in the office of the Vice President.

Vice President's Power to Act as President

Article 65 gives the president the authority to serve as president or discharge his duties in the event of a vacancy or in the absence of the president.

1. In the event of a vacancy in the office of the President due to his death, resignation, removal, or otherwise, the Vice President shall act as President until a new President is elected in accordance with the provisions of this chapter to fill the vacancy.
2. In the event that the President is unable to perform his duties due to absence, illness, or any other reason, the Vice President will perform those duties until the President resumes his duties.
3. The Vice President shall have all the powers and immunities of the President during and in respect of the period during which he is acting as or discharging the functions of President, and shall be entitled to such emoluments, allowances, and privileges as may be determined by Parliament by law, and until such provision is made, such emoluments, allowances, and privileges as are specified in the Second Schedule.

Ex-officio Chairman of Rajya Sabha

Article 64 and 89(1) of the Constitution of India talks about Vice President's role as ex-officio Chairman of the Council of States.

The Vice President shall be ex-officio Chairman of the Council of States and shall not hold any office of profit, Provided, however, that during any period in which the Vice President acts as President, he shall not perform the duties of the Chairman of the Council of States and shall be ineligible for any salary or allowance payable to the Chairman of the Rajya Sabha under Article 97.

1. The Vice President of India serves as the Council of States' ex-officio Chairman.
2. The Vice President is a member of the Executive branch of the government, but as Chairman of the Rajya Sabha, he also serves as a member of Parliament.

Dual Role of Vice President

The Vice President's office is one of the peculiar features of the Indian Constitution. Th Vice President would preside over the Upper house (Rajya Sabha) and act as President in certain contingencies. Thus, this way, the Vice President of India takes up this dual capacity. First as the second highest head of the Executive and secondly, as the Presiding officer of the Rajya Sabha of Parliament. The separation of powers says that no person should have two roles or positions in Government yet Vice President gets two distinct powers and offices.

This eventually causes huge burden of responsibility on the holder of the two offices. He is expected to keep the duties of the two offices distinct and separate as these are two critical roles which involve proper decision making. It is also to be noted that while performing duties as Vice President, one cannot take any decision that clashes with the other position or office of him. As difficult as it may appear, the individual must manage through the chair of the Council of States with exceptional distinction and perform their tasks with dignity and ease on their own. These roles receive admiration and appreciation from nation as a whole as it involves dual roles by a single person.

Conclusion

The position of Vice President is a significant position of all the offices in the country. His duty is vital to the nation and Government. The Constitution has defined provisions for election, term of office of Vice President and how he can be removed from the office. It also talks about the powers the Vice President exercises over two positions. His dual role as Vice President and Ex-officio Chairman is crucial to the nation as it requires distinctive skills. He receives immense admiration from the nation.

Author's Biography

I am Maranganty Sreelakshmi, a 2nd year passionate law student pursuing my law degree from Vivekananda Institute of Professional Studies from Indraprastha University, Delhi. I have great interest in writing legal articles to spread awareness among the people in the society.

CHAPTER SEVENTEEN

AN OVERVIEW OF THE MUSLIM WOMEN (PROTECTION OF RIGHTS ON MARRIAGE) ACT, 2019

Author: Sreeparna Bhattacharjee, IV year of B.A.,LL.B(Hons.) From Amity University, Kolkata.

Co-author: Dhriti Chanda, B.Com.,LL.B(Hons.) From Amity University, Kolkata.

INTRODUCTION

In Muslim law, "Triple Talaq" is a form of divorce in which a husband can give his wife divorce by saying "Talaq" three times in a succession. The presence of the aggrieved women is not mandatory; she can be given Talaq without providing a valid cause. Under Muslim law, the term "Talaq" refers to a husband's rejection of a marriage. Since ancient times, the practice of triple Talaq has been practised in India.

There are three kinds of talaq in Islam: Ahsan, Hasan, and Talaq-e-Biddat (triple or instant talaq). Biddat cannot be revoked, although Ahsan and Hasan can. Triple talaq is most commonly practised among India's Muslim community who adhere to the Hanafi Islamic school of law. By repeating the word "talaq" three times, a Muslim man can divorce his wife, while women are unable to speak the same and must seek divorce through the Sharia Act of 1937.

In India's legal history, the public movement to abolish talaq-e-biddat, or triple talaq, has a lengthy history. In the case of Shayara Bano v. Union of India and Anr (2017), the Supreme Court finally put a halt to the practice.

The aforementioned Act aims to safeguard the rights of Muslim women who are working to achieve the constitutional goals of Gender Justice and Equality. The Supreme Court declared the practice of triple talaq, where Muslim husbands can instantaneously and irrevocably divorce their wives by uttering the words 'talaq talaq talaq' as unconstitutional. So therefore, The Muslim Women (Protection of Rights on Marriage) Ordinance 2018 was passed by the President of India in 2018, making triple talaq not only void and unlawful, but also a non-bailable and cognizable offence punishable., The Parliament latter passed the Muslim Women (Protection of Rights on Marriage) Act, 2019 and hence the act was enforced.

BRIEFLY STATING THE PROVISIONS OF THE ACT

Section 1:- Extent and commencement

The Muslim Women (Protection of Rights on Marriage) Act, 2019 extends to the whole country of India and is deemed to have taken effect on September 19, 2018.

Section 2:- Definitions

Section 2 (a) states that electronic form is to be considered same as defined under section clause (r)of sub-section (1) of section 2 of the Information Technology Act, 2000. the act also states that "Magistrate" means a Judicial Magistrate of the First Class having jurisdiction under the Code of Criminal Procedure, 1973,in the region where the married Muslim women resides in order to avoid any complications. It is also defined under this section that "Talaq" denotes talaq-e-biddat or any other similar type of talaq having the impact of an instantaneous and irrevocable divorce declared by a Muslim husband.

Section 3:- . Talaq to be void and illegal

Any talaq declaration made by a Muslim husband against his wife, whether verbally, in writing, electronically, or in any other manner, is void and illegal.

Section 4:- Penalty

This provision provides that any Muslim husband who pronounces the Talaq described in section 3 is subject to a three-year prison sentence as well as a fine.

Section 5 – Allowance for maintenance

The magistrate determines that under this section, any married Muslim women upon whom Talaq has been exercised is entitled to receive subsistence allowance from her husband for her and the children.

Section 6 – Custody of the Children

In this section it is stated that in the event of Talaq of the married Muslim woman, the custody of her minor children is entitled to her for the time being and that will be determined by the magistrate.

Section 7 – Discretion of the magistrate

1. It shall be considered to be cognizable if any offence is punishable under this Act, if the facts relating to the commission of the offence is given to an Officer in charge of a police station by any person related to aggrieved women by blood or married Muslim women herself upon whom Talaq is held.
2. At the request of married Muslim women on whom Talaq is pronounced with the magistrate's authorization and terms and conditions, an offence punishable under this act may be compounded.
3. No bail can be granted by the magistrate unless the accused files an application, and the magistrate finds adequate grounds after hearing the married Muslim woman upon whom Talaq is pronounced, then bail can be granted as the magistrate deems fit.

Section 8 – The Muslim Women (Protection of Marriage Rights) Second Ordinance, 2019 has been repealed. and any action taken under the Muslim Women (Protection of Rights on Marriage) Second Ordinance, 2019 will be done so in accordance with the terms of this Act.

<u>**ISSUES AND CHALLEGES**</u>

The step of the Government to legislate the act is a positive one but some people are criticizing it and some of are in support of this particular decision. Some have also argued that It is obvious that the penalty imposed is unjust and unreasonable. Any Court of law dealing with family affairs must first attempt to reconcile the parties, but there is no such provision in the current act, nor is there any provision for mediation. However, the law is divisive since it criminalises the practise of talaq-i-biddat rather than just stating that a divorce granted in this manner is illegal. It means that any husband who performs triple-talaq, whether orally, in writing, or electronically, is likely to face a fine and a three-year prison sentence

Furthermore, how the husband is expected to support the wife while imprisoned is a critical question. It utterly negates the objective of the act, since the woman may be left financially destitute with no support for herself or her children, if any, and it may also prevent the woman to seek help from the act as she is afraid of her husband going to the prison after committing such an offence.Opponents see political evil at work, claiming that the government's eagerness to inflict criminal punishments is motivated by anti-Muslim sentiment. They claim that rather than defending women, the government's primary goal has been to threaten Muslim men who are terrified to be arrest.

CONCLUSION

The Act was drafted with good intentions, but there are several flaws that will need to be addressed and corrected over time. Because the Judicial Magistrate's position is so important because so much of the Act is based on his discretion, certain guiding considerations must be established.

The practicing of Triple Talaq has always been seen as a serious issue by the whole world, but there are few of Muslim countries have discontinued the practice of Triple Talaq, an extended time ago. Hopefully, the Act, via judicial precedents, will provide more clarity to its applications, remedies and the unwarranted situations that may arise due to the strict nature of the legislation

CHAPTER EIGHTEEN

PATENT LICENSING

Author: Salvee, IV Year of B.A.,LL.B from Bharati Vidyapeeth Deemed to be University, New Law School, Pune.

A patent is a limited right permitted for an innovation, which is a process that lay out, in general, a new method of doing something like a new practical solution to a problem. To acquire patent, technical details about the innovation must be revealed to the public in a patent application.

Licensing is explicated as a business disposition, in which a company sanctions another company by furnishing a license to transiently approach its intellectual property rights. A license is a compliance through which a licensee rents the rights to a legally secured block of intellectual property from a licensor.

WHAT IS PATENT LICENCING?

Patent licensing is an action of the third party in light of which, by process of selling and utilizing the patented patent, rights to withdraw its benefits. The possessor of the patent permits a third party to treat, sell and take benefit of its patented origination for a sum previously conferred as royalties. The license can be specified for a span of time as per the contract between patent owner and licensee. In the course of this time period, the license can utilize the patented invention and can take financial enjoyment.

According to section 68 of the patent act, 1970 for a patent license to be authentic, the contract must be in writing. As licensing is a deal between two parties where licensor admits the terms & conditions of the owner of the patent.

Licensing is determined as a contract therefore section 10 & 11 of IPA, 1970 will accompanied.

DIFFERENT TYPES OF PATENT LICENSING

There are 8 types of patent license: -

1. Exclusive Licensing: In this, all the rights beside title of the invention are provided to the licensee. Patent owner transmits the possession of the patent to the licensee. Patent owner has only acquired the title of the invention. Thus, licensee obtains all the duties related to the invention. However, licensee cannot allow the patent to anyone else. It is solely permitted to him/her; thus, licensee is the only certified person to utilize the patented invention.

2. Non-exclusive licensing: In a non-exclusive right, the licensee has the right to sell and construct the patented design, but such right is not unique. Patent owner may give approval to utilize and build such patented model to any other person also. In this case, all of them have the right to construct, utilize and sell the patented design. The rights exalt by this license are not unique to a specific licensee.

3. Sub license: In this process, the licensee has the right to issue a license to a distinct association for the manufacturing of the product. In other words, the licensee has the right to give the license to the third party who has the advantage to create the product. However, the profits will depend on the contract between the primary licensee and the third party.

4. Cross licensing: It is the interchange of license between different association and makers. When invention needs the reinforcement of other products to make its place in the market.

5. Voluntary Licensing: An action of goodness towards the society. It is also appropriate for medicinal patents. In this licensing, patent owner can license his patented invention to other parties on exclusive or non-exclusive basis and offer right to production, construction or administer a medicinal product. According to the contract, licensee can sale and allocate the product in a market. The owner of the patent gets its kingship as per the terms & conditions given in the contract.

6. Compulsory licensing: In compulsory licensing, the consent is given to a third party to create, utilize or sell a patented invention without the clearance of the owner of the patent. As per section 84 & 92 of the Indian Patent Act, 1970, if the stated conditions are fulfilled, license can be conceded to a third party without the sanction of the patent owner. According to the Section 84 of IPA, 1970, any person who is engrossed or already the possessor of the license under the patent can appeal to the controller for allowance of mandatory license after 3 years from the date of permit of that patent.

The patent office examines the essence of the invention, caliber of the candidate to use the invention for the public interest, any step so far taken by the licentiates to make complete utilization of the invention and time transpire from permit of the patent. Compulsory licensing is generally engaged for treatment of patents. Government grant someone to exercise patented invention, to construct, utilize or sell patented invention without taking consent of patent owner for public welfare.

7. Carrot licensing: In this the licensing perspective is advisable when the possible licensee is not in the exercise of the patented invention and does not fall under any commitment to take a license. This sort of license is a marketing strategy where the patent owner offers the license a sight of what could be achieved by obtaining a license for their patent. In other words, it is clearly a market practice in which you assure an expected licensee to take a license.

8. Stick licensing: It is another view point of licensing which is thoroughly disparity of the carrot licensing. In this licensing, awaited licensee is ahead using the patented technology and thus violating the patent. The patent owner can file litigation against the invader or settle with the invader accepting to license his patent.

<u>ADVANTAGES AND DISADVANTAGES OF PATENT LICENSING</u>
ADVANTAGES

For the owner of the patent, the licensing pattern suggests the following advantages:

- There is no need to observe money to advertise the product – the license will be answerable for costs of fabricating, dispensation, wrapping, purchasing & sales etc.
- Can grow your inventions faster ion the market – if you issue a license to an entrenched business, it will be easy for you to grasp their experience, armature & collusion. They will commonly be more able to pass your product into the marketplace more effortlessly and rapidly.
- Will be able to create profits – the license will reimburse for the right to grasp the license to your patent.
- One can split into two markets – based on the agreement and the license, you may be able to acquire markets that are limited to imports, avert export taxes or diminish risks related international enlargements.
- Can keep possession of your intellectual property – licensing allows you to give distribute, challengers or supporting business specific rights over

your patent while receiving royalty income and still keeping possession of your asset.

DISADVANTAGE

- Loss of control – for the interval of license, the patent owner shifts his rights to the license. Consequence of which is he drop his own control, either moderately or wholly on his own invention.
- Difficulty in regulating licensee – it takes lots of endeavor and time to ascertain the suitable licensee for the invention. It is necessary to get a potential licensee and have a organized contract in command to have the greatest possibility of success.
- Risk of licensee's ability – the patent owner depends on the coherence and capacity of the licensee to efficiently advertise the patent product. The fear of poor plan and quality management can resentfully influence the patent character & achievement.

LICENSING UNDER INDIAN PATENT ACT

Section 84 to 92 of IPA 1970 are associate to patent licensing. As per IPA 1970, patent licensing should be in writing between the licensor and the licensee. Section 84 of IPA 1970, affirm the terms and conditions needed for issuing compulsory licensing. The act has the amenities and authorize the controller to issue the compulsory licensing to the third party.

Compulsory licensing is feasible only if the patented formulation is beneficial to public health or in national emergencies or health disaster. According to the section 84 of the IPA 1970, after 3 years from the permit of the patent, any intrigued person can write an appeal to the controller for permit of compulsory license on the following grounds:

1. The logical necessity of the public for the patented formulation have not been triumphant.
2. Patented formulation is not accessible to the public in economical price.
3. Patented formulation is not performed within the domain of India.

After receiving the appeal, the controller can permit a compulsory license to the party.

However, prior to permitting the compulsory license, the controller has to contemplate various components such as:

1. Authority/remittance for the patented are equitable.
2. License will apply patented formulation properly.
3. Patented formulation will be accessible to the public at affordable prices.
4. The license is generic & inalienable.
5. The license will not be prolonged than the duration of the patent.
6. Licensing the patented formulation is for the finer contribution in Indian market.
7. If patented formulation is for semi-conductor mechanics, the license permitted is for charitable public benefit.

Compulsory license can be permitted to a medication products & exports of specific medication products that are mandatory for public health of a country having fragile magnitude of medication industry can be granted.

DIFFERENCE BETWEEN PATENT LICENSE AND PATENT ASSIGNMENT

Patent license can be introduced to be an act of the patent holder where he gives approval to withdraw advantage on interests on the patent to a third party for a restricted duration. Such transfer of rights is interim in essence. In patent license, the licensee is required to reimburse the authority to the licensor for the whole term of the license period.

Whereas, in patent assignment, patent holder assigns unique rights of the patent to a third party for forever. Such a transfer is documented in the official patent record. In patent assignment, the assignee has to reimburse the lump sum amount to the patent owner in the starting and later can collect surplus from the patented formulation.

Patent Assignment is an absolute transfer of rights to a third party. Patent owner don't have any rights on his patented formulation once patent is transferred to a third party.

LIMITATIONS OF PATENT LICENSING

Licensing is a very easy way for a patent holder to take monetary assistance from a patented formulation.

Few limitations of licensing are as follows:

1. Licensing could be less beneficial. It may happen that if the patent holder makes the formulation accessible in market, it can attain more gain than license. Though investing funds is a risk, but gain can be more than presumption.

2. Patent holder has to rely upon the licensee for gains. Patent holder is completely dependent on the licensee, his sources, his skills and the attempt for marketing the patented formulation and further for monetary welfare. Thus, if an actual license is not chosen, then the product may get abort in the market.

3. A compliance of licensing should be inducted very carefully. All the terms & conditions associated to authority and further rectification should be declared distinctly in the agreement. Also, agreement should distinctly states all the sections associated to assets and details associated to patented formulation.

4. The license has to recompense fixed rank to the patent holder disregarding of the positions of the product in the market.

CONCLUSION

Patent licensing refers to granting authorization to a third party for utilizing patented innovation. Patent holder can get fine monetary welfare by licensing his patented innovation. As per Indian Patent Act, 1970 patent licensing should be in written format and persuade the subsections stated in section 84 to 94 of IPA, 1970. The license agreement is between two parties, one is licensee & other is patent holder or licensor. Slightly protection should be taken while choosing the licensee and formulating the accordance.

CHAPTER NINETEEN

PREAMBLE TO THE INDIAN CONSTITUTION

Author: Anushka Bagri, II year of B.A.,LL.B from Banasthali vidyapith.

The term preamble refers to the introduction or preface. With respect to the constitution, it is the introduction of constitution or summary of the constitution. The American Constitution was the first such constitution in the world which has adopted the terminology called preamble.

In words of N.A. Palkhivala, an eminent jurist preamble is an identity card of the constitution. The preamble to the Indian Constitution is based on the Objective Resolution drafted and moved by Pt. Jawaharlal Nehru and adopted by Constituent Assembly.

The preamble to the Constitution of India is a brief introductory statement that sets out the guiding purpose, principles and philosophy of the constitution. Preamble gives an idea about the following:

(1) The Source of the Constitution: - The Preamble states that the constitution derives its authority from the people of India

(2) Nature of Indian State: - It declares India to be of a sovereign, socialist, secular, democratic, and republican polity.

(3) Objectives of the Constitution: - It specifies justice, liberty, equality, and fraternity as the objectives.

(4) Date of adoption of the Constitution: - It stipulates November 26, 1949, as the date of adoption.

KEY WORDS IN THE PREAMBLE

There are certain key words in the preamble of Indian Constitution such as Sovereign, Socialist, Secular, Democratic, Republic, Justice, Liberty, Equality, and Fraternity.

SOVEREIGN: - This word sovereign basically means supreme. It implies that India has its own independent authority and it is not a dominion of any other external power. In the country, the legislature has the power to make laws. There is no authority above it, and it is free to conduct its own affairs (both internal and external). Becoming a member of Commonwealth of Nations or United Nation Organization doesn't affect the sovereignty of India.

SOCIALIST: This term was added by the 42nd Constitutional Amendment Act, 1976. It means the achievement of socialist ends through democratic means. It holds faith in a mixed economy where both private and public sectors co-exist side by side. This indicates that Indian brand of socialism is a democratic socialism.

But before the addition of this word in Preamble the constitution already had a socialist content in the form of certain Directive Principles of State Policies.

In case of Excel Wear v/s Union of India, Supreme Court held that the addition of word "socialist" in preamble might enable the courts to lean more in favor of nationalism and State ownership of an industry.

SECULAR: - This term was added by the 42nd Constitutional Amendment Act of 1976. It means that all the religions in India get equal respect, protection and support from the state. Before the addition of this word also, the constitution consists of such provisions (Articles 25 to 28) which indicate that India is a Secular state or the makers of the constitution wanted India to be a Secular State.

In S. R. Bommai v/s Union of India case, the Supreme Court has held that "secularism" is the basic feature of the Indian Constitution.

DEMOCRATIC: - This term implies that the Constitution of India has an established form of Constitution which gets its authority from the will of the people expressed in an election. This term indicates the nature of government India has i.e., India is a Democratic State.

REPUBLIC: - A democratic nation can be divided into two categories i.e., monarchy and republic. In a monarchy, the head of state is usually a king or a queen. And in republic, the head of the state is always an elected head by direct or indirect elections for a fixed term. India is a republic nation which means that its head is not a hereditary one but an elected i.e., President is the head of Indian State and he is an indirectly elected body.

JUSTICE: - It is necessary to maintain order in society that is promised through various provisions of Fundamental Rights and Directive Principles of State Policy provided by the Constitution of India. It comprises three elements, which is social, economic, and political.

1. Social Justice – Social justice means that the Constitution wants to create a society without discrimination on any grounds like caste, creed, gender, religion, etc.
2. Economic Justice – Economic Justice means no discrimination can be caused by people on the basis of their wealth, income, and economic status. Every person must be paid equally for an equal position and all people must get opportunities to earn for their living.
3. Political Justice – Political Justice means all the people have an equal, free and fair right without any discrimination to participate in political opportunities.

EQUALITY: The term 'Equality' means no section of society has any special privileges and all the people have given equal opportunities for everything without any discriminations. Everyone is equal before the law.

LIBERTY: The term 'Liberty' means freedom for the people to choose their way of life, have political views and behavior in society. Liberty does not mean freedom to do anything, a person can do anything but, in the limit, set by the law.

FRATERNITY: The term 'Fraternity' means a feeling of brotherhood and an emotional attachment with the country and all the people. Fraternity helps to promote dignity and unity in the nation.

IMPORTANCE OF PREAMBLE

In reBerubari Case, the Supreme Court held that Preamble is a key to open the mind of the makers, and shows general purpose for which they made the several provisions in the Constitution.

According to Sir Alladi Krishnaswami Iyer, "Preamble to our constitution expresses what we had thought or dreamt so long".

PREAMBLE AS A PART OF INDIAN CONSTITUTION

The preamble being part of the Constitution is discussed several times in the Supreme Court. It can be understood by reading the following two cases. In Berubari's case the Supreme Court held that the Preamble was not a part of the Constitution and therefore it could not be regarded as a source of any substantive powers. In Kesavananda Bharati's Case, Supreme Court overruled its earlier judgement and held that Preamble is the Part of the Constitution.

AMENDMENT OF THE PREAMBLE

As in case of Kesavananda Bharati it was held that preamble is integral part of constitution. Then as a part of the Constitution, preamble can be amended under Article 368 of the Constitution, but the preamble contains the basic elements or the fundamental features of the constitution. These basic elements or features cannot be destroyed or damaged by amendments. As of now, the preamble is only amended once through the 42nd Amendment Act, 1976.

CONCLUSION

As from all the above points it can be concluded that preamble is the integral part of Indian Constitution. And it can be amended as any other part of constitution but its basic features cannot be destroyed. Also, preamble states objectives of the constitution makers as well as it is a key to open the minds of constitutional makers. And lastly it states the basic nature of Indian Constitution.

CHAPTER TWENTY

UNDERSTANDING THE LAW AND SOCIETY THROUGH THE CASE MOHAMMED MUSHTAQ GK V. AYESHA BANU

Author: Palak Rastogi, I year of B.A.,LLB (Hons.) From NMIMS School Of Law.

INTRODUCTION

Karnataka High Court's verdict on Mohammad Mushtaq GK v. Ayesha Banu seems reasonably sound but not socially progressive. The court's attitude towards women, especially mothers are a misogynist in this case. Conflating the attributes of a 'good' mother with the biological mother is highly contentious in this case. Demonizing the stepmother in the statement given by the court is morally and socially alarming even when the court tries to act sensitively towards the biological mother. Reading between the lines of the case will reveal how legally sound verdicts could also be patriarchal in nature. This case is evident enough of the patriarchal mentality of the court where motherhood is innate and instinctive rather than conditioned by societal norms. This case law focuses both on the social institution and social group as a major part of society.

The case explores the legal affinities linked with the family and marriage as the social institutions and women as a paramount social group in humankind. The objective is to study the judgement given by the Karnataka High Court to understand the cause for the legal battle between the estranged spouses for the custody of a minor child and also to familiarize with the biased perception regarding the 'Motherhood' existing in the Indian society.

The Judgement of the case is given by Justice Krishna S Dixit. One of the things he does well is problematising the issues of a family linked with marriage in society by dismissing a petition challenging the order of a Family Court in Bangalore, denying the father for custody of the minor child but according to the visitation rights.

The background of the case showcases the petitioner–husband as employed in a renowned MNC namely Honeywell Technology Solutions, Bangalore. His nikah was solemnized on 30.4.2009 in Bangalore with Ayesha Bano and a child was born on 1.8.2013 named Mohammed Shahraan Hussain. Because of the apparent temperamental differences, the marriage broke down and the wife as the respondent filed a suit for dissolution of the marriage. In the same course of time, the petitioner had married another woman according to the Muslim Personal Law and was residing with her and had a child with her as well. He admitted to living a happy life with his new wife.

BRIEF FACTS OF THE CASE

The plea was filed by the petitioner contending that he was in a better position to take care of the child from a financial perspective and provide the child with the best upbringing, education, and a complete family environment. It was also the petitioner's contention that the respondent (biological mother) had neglected her duties towards the minor child and the petitioner before. The single-judge also stated that an affidavit from the second wife that she would take care of the child would be of little solace to the biological mother.

KEY QUESTIONS ADDRESSED BY THE KARNATAKA HIGH COURT

- "In a society like ours, the disputes concerning child custody by their very nature are complex, no matter religion or faith to which the parties belong."
- Mother, step-mother & child: What if the custody was given to the petitioner, the mother would end up all alone while the petitioner will live with the child and a wife.
- What reasons recognizes the need for a writ petition to be filed under articles 226 and 227 of the Constitution of India praying for interim custody of the child by the court.

Similar case law to substantiate the above-mentioned case was delivered by Madras High court in 1911 used as a reference point to articulate the misandrist views in the society. In this regard, the Karnataka High Court placed reliance on a judgment of the TN. Muthuveerappa Chetty vs. T.R. Ponnuswami Chetty which held the following:

"It does not appear that, excepting the respondent's wife, there is any female relation living with him competent to take proper care of the child. It would be hardly safe to presume that his wife, the child's stepmother, would be willing to do so... There is good reason for believing that the maternal relations have a strong affection for the child."

Madras High Court's assumption about motherhood begins and ends with a biological mother. Such judgements as reference points for justice as used by Karnataka High Court leads to more orthodox and socially regressive thinking in the society.

Karnataka High court leaves no stone unturned to justify their insistence on the direct relationship between biological mother and affection for the child. Of the extracts from the poem listed by the judge to demonstrate what a biological mother means to a child that cannot be better explained than by quoting "To My Mother" (1849) the poem penned by an American poet Edgar Allan Poe:

Because I feel that, in the Heavens above,

The angels, whispering to one another,

Can find, among their burning terms of love,

None so devotional as that of 'Mother'...

This poem portrays how the stepmother is denied fair treatment by the court on the grounds of 'ideal motherhood' and by giving more solace and consolation to the biological mother within the tightly-policed circle of the patriarchal regime, held up by Judge S Dixit as a historical sign of disrespect for women in the community.

The Verdict on Mohammad Mushtaq GK v. Ayesha Banu 2021 summoned by paternal mindset firmly revolves around the vision of 'Ideal Motherhood' by stating, "Stepmothers would not ordinarily be able to take care of and show affection to children which biological mothers instinctively would, the Karnataka High Court recently observed while denying interim custody of a child to the father on the ground that he had remarried."Additionally, the Court opined that the idea that if the custody of the child was given to the petitioner, the respondent would be all alone and the petitioner would have two children at his hands along with the second wife "offends the very sense of justice, to say the least."

The decision pronounced by the court can per se sounds legally competent but lacks in fulfilling the societal cause. The burden of such a phobic attitude towards mothers is suffered by women in society in general, which is the reason why we experience "The Shame." in understanding that, being a biological mother does not fulfil the ideal criteria to shed the love and warmth needed as a mother. The verdict by the Karnataka High Court stands absurd and vague in defining the role of a mother based on a biological identity.

The picture used by the court uses silhouettes to depict the relation of a mother and child. Silhouettes as a visual model of depiction do not discriminate against different kinds of mothers. Love and affection between the mother and child matter the most. However, the verdict by court says otherwise and assumes that stepmothers are less affectionate than biological mothers.

The controversial judgement made by the Karnataka High Court has a significant Social Impact by targeting women as a crucial part of social groups in India:

- "Being a mother is biological but motherhood is the construction of a social identity and it falls under a part of common procedure as a family.", the judgement solely fails to highlight the importance of the mother-child relationship in society rather than focuses on the types of mothers.
- The judgement affirms enmity among women where a woman is assumed to think ill of the other women and they are always enemies to each other. Also, lacks the social concern regarding the biased decision given by the court on questioning motherhood and their affinities towards children.
- The discriminatory element used by the court and by arguing that the social status of the women does not provide behavioural impunity, the court was also unsuccessful to recognise the sentiments of women in the society as a whole even behind seemingly respectable facades.
- More precisely, the court's attitude towards the marriage, in this case, is also unjust to the spouse, by only considering the relation of a child with the biological mother and consequently, ignoring the petitioner's i.e father's love and affection towards the child.
- The judgement is mostly an account of the arguments made by the court that fails to cover the flaws and also reflects the absence of socially appropriate behaviour towards women and especially mothers so far.

As a result, the judgement may stand legally correct but for sure is socially regressive. This is a welcome intervention in a country and a legal profession that is intensely hierarchical, stratified and paternalistic with women inevitably ending up at the bottom of the pile. The Karnataka High court may try to use emotions as a means to share solidarity with mothers but breaks down the reasonability needed by the court to promote social significance bypassing the decision in the regard to women. In Conclusion, these judgments have a great social impact on society and no decision should defame the special social groups and social institutions that exist in humankind. The Karnataka High court intends to issue writs under Art 226, but cannot turn blind eye to the biased decision against women and specifically targeting mothers in the society.

Author's Biography

This is Palak, a first-year student pursuing Law. My academic interests include Jurisprudence, Commercial Law and Criminal Law. I willingly wish to explore other avenues in the field of law throughout my LLB journey. I am a quick and keen learner and am always looking for new opportunities in the newly emerging areas of legal research and writing.

CHAPTER TWENTY-ONE

THE IMPERATIVENESS OF ENFORCING MORE STRINGENT ANIMAL WELFARE LAWS IN INDIA

Author: Anmol Gupta, III Year of B.B.A.,LL.B from Symbiosis Law School, Hyderabad.

"If Animals Spoke, Humanity would cry.

-Manuj Rajput

Humanity would collectively cry in shame if they begin to face the reality of humans torturing animals – and if the voiceless creatures start talking back. Like humans, animals have the anatomy whose functionality depends on the circulatory system spearheaded by the functioning of the heart, they too can feel things and they all need food and shelter to survive. The most notable difference between the two species is that humans can express their thoughts while animals cannot.

So, is humanity a characteristic native to only sentient beings that survive on two feet? Is this criteria enough for animals to suffer? And the most important question is - who sets these criteria to differentiate one living being from another? And is this criteria viable and enforceable under law?

Every living being – irrespective of their genealogy – has a right to live with peace and dignity, be it an animal or a human and 'no person/ entity' can dare to take this right away from them. We do have laws in place in our Constitution to protect these rights within the boundaries of our country but what good is a law if not executed properly and what good it is if people are not aware of it? Knowledge about the laws and rights of the animals are very important because we humans tend to treat animals like they are lifeless creatures and with increasing cruelty towards these animals be it mental, physical or destroying their habitats have often resulted in extinction of various species and the day is not far when we see lab-grown and/or reanimated animals in society.

Legislative and Judicial Stand

Article 51A (g) of the Indian Constitution defines our fundamental duty to protect and improve the environment "including wildlife". We have seen cases where people carelessly destroy forests or pollute water bodies and once such case is that of the defacing of the Yamuna floodplains by The Art of Living Foundation during a three-day celebration. The damage to Yamuna Floodplains was so severe that as per reports it lost almost all its natural vegetation and which was home to a large number of animals. AoL was subsequently admonished by the National Green Tribunal in June 2017 for not following environment protection norms and was fined Rs. 42 crores for their mishandling of the situation. Furthermore, to protect and improve our wildlife it is very important to teach the importance of the survivability of animals on our life from the beginning, which the Apex court kept in mind while deciding in the case of M.C Mehta v U.O.I. The court held that, "it is the duty of the Central Government to direct all the educational institutions of our country to teach and train citizens about the protection and improvement of the environment for at least one hour a week."

Post-Independence, the first ever legislation made for the protection of wildlife was 'The Prevention of Cruelty to Animals Act, 1960.' The main object of this legislation was to stop animal cruelty and to prohibit and deter any person, be it the owner of the animal or caretaker from inflicting or causing pain or suffering to any animal. Any act of beating, kicking, torturing, mutilating, administering injurious substances or killing of an animal was made a crime and even over- riding, over- driving, over- loading an animal was made illegal. This legislation intended to cover various acts of injustice and cruelty on animals and made it an illegal and punishable offence. In the case of N.R Nair and Ors. V U.O.I the Kerala H.C was of the opinion that the training and exhibition of 5 animals namely - dogs, panthers, tigers, monkeys and bears, should be banned as this also amounts to cruelty on such animals. The court held that, "circus animals are being forced to perform unnatural tricks, are housed in cramped cages. Subjected to fear, hunger, and pain, not to mention the undignified way of life they have to live with no respite...Though not homosapiens they are also beings entitled to dignified existences and humane treatment sans cruelty and torture." Even the practice of Jallikattu- bull fighting was banned by the S.C in the case of Animal Welfare Board of India v. A Nagaraja and Ors for violating sections 3 and 11 of PCA Act, 1960.

Another legislation drafted was the Wildlife Protection Act of 1972. This legislation was enacted with the intent to prohibit hunting of wild animals, protect creatures on a verge of extinction, to specify animals that can be hunted. Killing wildlife animals is illegal but killing them to protect or in good faith is seen as an exception, this was held by the S.C in the case of Tilak Bahadur Rai v. St of A.P where a man shot tiger to death to protect himself.

Except these legislations, the animals are also protected under Sec. 428 and Sec. 429 of the Indian Penal Code. Sec. 428 of IPC punishes any person who commits mischief by killing, poisoning or maiming any animal of the value of ten rupees or upwards with imprisonment up to 2 years or fine or both. Whereas, Sec 429 of IPC punishes any person for committing the same mischief with any elephant, camel, horse mule, buffalo, bull, cow or ox or any other animal of the value of Rs. 50 or more with imprisonment up to 5 years or fine or both. In the case of State Of Bihar vs Murad Ali Khan the S.C was of the opinion that in case of double jeopardy "then the offender shall be liable to be prosecuted and punished under either or any of those enactments, but shall not be liable to be punished twice for the same offence."

<u>Conclusion</u>

India has various legislations and sections enacted to protect animals. Laws have never been a problem in this case. The main problem is enforcing these laws and educating people about these laws. The discrepancy between laws and their implementation results in inability to provide effective solutions. According to statistics, India slaughters 16 land base animals per person/ year and is given "C" rating under Animal Protection Index (API) and moderate performer under Sanctioning Cruelty Category and according to another statistics in India there are 138 police officers per lakh of population making India the fifth lowest amongst the 71 countries.This explains the ineffectiveness of laws in India. India being one of the largest country and Second largest countries in terms of population makes it very difficult for the police officers to guide and enforce these laws. This makes educating people about the laws more important because only when they are aware of these laws, they will file complaint and stand up for any mis-happening that takes place. Educating people should start from the ground level, from the schools and at home, parents should teach their child to protect and care for animals and not torture them. Only when these kids are aware of their duties and laws and punishment that comes along if these laws are violated, it is only then they will stand up for their rights and for the rights of others as well, helping India to be a better nation.

CHAPTER TWENTY-TWO

THE PRESENT SCENARIO OF CORPORATE GOVERNANCE IN INDIA

Author: Ananya Alok, III year of B.B.A.,LL.B from Banasthali Vidyapith, Jaipur, Rajasthan.

ABSTRACT

The term corporate is basically basically taken from the Latin term corpus which means body, and the term governance implies the meaning of instructing the frameworks and procedures to fulfill the desire of a partner. In today's business and corporate world the term 'corporate governance' is a system by which a company is administrated , controlled and directed by a set of corporate process, law , customs and policies. India's corporate governance structure contains a scope of measures that generates or advances the responsibility of governance and straight forwardness of money related and other data. Moreover , the concept of corporate social responsibility has greatly focused on the concept of corporate governance for incorporating social and environmental concerns for the decision making process of the business, which will benefit not only investors (financial investors) but also to the communities , employees and consumers. In the current scenario, the corporate governance is being mostly connected with business practices and public policies that are stakeholders and shareholders friendly.

There are many changes done from the past and the present scenario regarding the concept of corporate governance by Indian government. The changes done were because of the reason of lack of management's responsibility. They lack not only towards shareholders, but also towards the public society at a large. At present the scenario, corporations are examined to be a social platform or we can say institution, which communicates with the society in many ways and affects the individuals of that society at a large. The system of corporate governance also includes the entire matrix of informal and formal interactions and relations between the member of board, shareholders, management, auditors, and other major interested parties. These kind of relations and interactions determine that how a company is governed and how risk factors returns from the corporate sector activities are determined. The present research paper will go for checking the concept of regulatory laws of corporate governance which is not given in a comprehensive manner and the rules, regulations etc. do not provide basic or standard norms or codes for the establishment and development of good corporate governance. We will basically study various kinds of research papers and books provided in the library to right this research paper. Mainly we will refer to the companies act 2013 and 1956 in the context of corporate governance structure. Which will helps us to mainly improve the understanding of laws and legal regulations regarding corporate governance in India at a glance.

INTRODUCTION

Corporate governance is basically a creation which reinforces the long term supportable value for the stakeholders through socially driven business process. Corporate governance covers a wide range of disciplines and it is also known as multidisciplinary field of study. Law, management, finance, ethics, consulting, economics and accounting. The main function to be performed by it is to provide the description of the advantages and duty of the shareholders and organizations. In case if failure (disagreements) occurs due to conflict among members, it is the authority of corporate governance to bring everyone again together. It also contains the basic purpose of setting the standards against which the work can be administrated. Good corporate governance provides the maximization of the value of shareholders ethically, legally and on a sustainable basis.

In ancient times the theory was given in two contexts, the Anglo American and the continental European context. Anglo American was known to be as dispersed ownership, short term equity finance, strong shareholders rights, flexible labor markets and active markets for capital control. Second is continental European which is known to be as concentrated block holder ownership, inactive markets for capital control, weak shareholders rights, long term debt financing and rigid labor markets. No country around the whole world can adopt either fully Anglo American policies or purely continental European system. To follow the policies of any one of the ancient system of corporate governance, we should go through from the various factors such as world presence, globalization, deregulation, competition etc. Which basically decides to what extent any country should adopt any of the two systems.

The TATA group and Infosys limited were the best illustration of corporate governance in past, which had ill-famed its reputation in society due to recent issues. The board room issues of high profile of two large corporate companies in India have evaluated the desire for transparency and ensuring that the interest of minority of the shareholders should be safeguard. In the case of Infosys Company limited, the so called founders of that company fall for the values which were already established and were not considered and followed in a certain remarkable decisions. The case of TATA company is of basically interrogating or we can say change the decisions of the erstwhile chairman of the company who carry's on to be as the controller of the shareholding trusts, and seems to have a lack of clear board processes to the issues reasonably and addressment of situations that will consider the reversal of decisions or even criteria of changing decisions between its economic and social part.

<u>LEGAL FRAMEWORK AND REGULATORY LAWS OF CORPORATE GOVERNANCE IN INDIA</u>

The concept of corporate governance in India, mainly arrived from the time period of economic liberalization and also from the de-regularization of business and industries. The development of corporate laws in India had been marked by the interesting contracts. The securities and exchange board of India and the ministry of corporate affairs laid on emphasis on each and every subject of importance by setting up various committees by the industry and by the examination of the reports and recommendations to the corporate governance.

The years since the time period of liberalization, it had proved the wide ranging of changes in rules, regulations and laws of driving corporate governance. It is noticeable from the various regulatory and legal frameworks and also from the committees which were set up for the corporate performance. Such regulatory frameworks, laws and guidance of the committees are as provided below:-

1. The corporate affair in India is basically regulated through the companies' act 1956 and the companies' act 2013 and even other allied

acts, rules and bill. It also provides or we can say renders many important services to shareholders and stakeholders. It also plays a crucial role in protecting the investors. The MCA (ministry of corporate affairs), government of India performs this crucial task. It also prohibits the adverse competition through competition act, 2002 and also elevates and sustains competition.

2. The company's law board is a quasi-judicial body which was established under company's act 1956. It regulates its own procedures and it also has power to do that.

3. The fraud investigation department: - it is an interdisciplinary organization which investigates financial serious frauds. It also investigates mainly those investigations, which involves public interest, and are multidisciplinary in nature and consists many other factors too.

4. The securities contract regulation act 1956:- it basically refers all types of government documents (tradable papers), stocks, bonds, shares, debentures and other marketable instruments or we can say securities issued by the companies. The code and conduct of stock exchange including its powers and parameters is defined by the securities contract regulation act 1956.

5. The securities exchange and board of India: - it encourages to the expansion of the securities in the market. It also even exhibits the unfair and fraudulent trade practices relating to the securities of market and even also manages the securities market and related conflicts with it. The main and basic function of securities and exchange board of India is to secure the interest of investors in securities.

6. The registrar of companies: - it basically serves with the primary objective of registration of companies and it also ensures that such kind of companies should comply with the statutory specifications under the act. It basically formed or we can say comes under the company's act 1956nsparently. There doesn't seems to have been an agreed formula at the top board level for the

7. Enforcement directorate: - It basically falls under the ministry of finance. It is very specialized investigating agency which helps in the implementation of foreign exchange and management act (FEMA) and also helps in the elimination of money laundering act (PMCA). The PMCA is a criminal law, where the empowerment of offices are done in order to conduct queries to find out the location of attach assets.

SIGNIFICANCE

- The objectives are set through the enhancement of structures which is done when there is better corporate governance or by the help of a good corporate governance structure. The means of achieving such objectives are checked properly and the production is basically monitored.
- The corporate governance also maintains a link between the company's financial reporting systems with the company's management.
- It also helps in shaping the future and the growth of capital markets of the economy.
- It makes management creative in order to take innovative and creative decisions which help in the efficient functioning of the corporation within its legal frame work.
- Safe and sound governance practices also used to make a contribution to the investor's self confidence in corporations and motivate them to stimulate long term capital.
- Good governance also improves the international reputation of the corporate sector and also helps to raise the global capital with the help of home companies.
- It also adds to the wealth of the economy and also enhances the effectiveness and the efficiency of the company .Thus, corporate governance is also known as the instrument of economic growth.
- Good corporate governance also supplies sufficient and timely disclosure of reporting requisites, and code of conduct to the companies. Along with this it also helps to avoid the insider trading. Insider trading refers to when companies used to present material and price sensitive details to outsiders and also ensures that till this detail is made social, the insiders and the employees present in the organization abstains from dealing in corporate securities.
- It also provides good support system to investors by allowing all the corporate accounting practices clear to them. A corporate enterprise also reveals the financial reporting structures in order to do that.

PRIME FUNDAMENTALS OF CORPORATE GOVERNANCE

After the major discussions held on the topic of corporate governance, it tends to refer the three principles raised in the important documents published since 1990:-

- The principles of corporate governance (OECD, 1998 and 2004)
- The Cadbury report (UK, 1992)
- The sarbanes-oxley act (2002)

The Sarbanes - Oxley act is attempts by the legislative asembly of United States in order to regulate several principles provided in the Cadbury and OECD reports. The OECD and Cadbury report basically represents the general principles through which the business operates to guarantee proper good corporate governance. Some of the principles are laid down below

1. The proper role and authority of the board: - The board requires appropriate level and adequate size of commitment and independence. It also needs applicable skills and sufficient comprehension to challenge the management performances.
2. Ethical behavior and integrity: - institutions should establish a basic code of conduct for their executive and director employees those who promotes in the responsible and ethical decision making And there should always be one factor present in mind to appointing the board members and corporate officers that is ' integrity '.
3. Equitable and right treatment of the shareholders: - Organizations can provide help to the shareholders in order to use their indemnity by openly communicating information and also by the encouragement of shareholders so that they can involve in the general convocations.
4. The interest of other stakeholders :- institutions should understand and acknowledge that they do contains legitimate , social , legal , and market driven accountability to non - shareholder and stakeholders which also includes investors , employees , local communities , benificiary , suppliers , policy makers and clients.
5. Transparency and disclosure: - There should be proper disclosure of matters to concerning the organization and should also be balanced and timely in order to ensure that each and every investors has an access to clear, factual information.

THE NEED AND THE REQUIRMENT OF CORPORATE GOVERNENCE IN INDIA

In this era the rapid pace of globalization had made more need for the emergence of corporate governance in India. Due to this the national governments and firms requires some fundamental changes because corporate governance is clearly very effective and beneficiary for the firms and countries .corporations must have to change the scenario and the way in which they operate . Even the national government must also maintain and establish the proper institutional code and conduct for it. Even there are no longer restrictions are made to the activities that are public listed in the organizations present in advanced industrial economies.

Through the means of high profile corporate scandals and public attention, the board of corporations and regulatory framework has forced governments to strictly consider the fundamental issues regarding the corporate governance as an essential element for the public monetary interest. Eventually the violate and instable experience of the emergence of markets in recent times have made an observation to the corrupt maladministration and practices in the international and national systems on public expenditure.

It has been clearly seen that inefficient management practices can leads to various business collapses and financial crisis around the world .these financial crisis and business collapses have made the business world to basically think and even to make a pressure upon the importance of safe and sound perspective of corporate governance practices. It has also been seen that the investors who invests in the organization are even ready to pay the higher amount of premiums for those companies who have safe and sound corporate governance structure and practices. Recently it could be seen that the international or global lenders have understand the importance of corporate governance practices as on the economic production of the companies and even also felt that the issues regarding corporate governance bears more significance and Importance while regarding taking the investment decisions into the account . A safe and sound and an effective corporate governance practice also provides an edge to the companies to raise funds at low level cost of capital , prevents any financial collapses and potential to overcome from it , enhances the standing position in the market and also helps in improving the liquidity position and financial soundness of a company .

A good corporate governance practice also improves the country's reputation and image by preventing the outflow of funds and by increasing the foreign capital flow. It also helps in increasing the strengthens and competitive power of the capital markets and finally increasing the chances of more prosperity by reducing and preventing the occurrence of any kind of financial crisis' and along with that it also helps in leading of the efficient allocation of resources . Various professors and by studying at an large extent have recommended that there is no single model of the corporate governance which could be compatible to each and every country in the world has constructed on the principles of equality , responsibility , transparency, and accountability which may be accepted widely and internationally for the corporate governance structure .The term know as equality could be defined as the equal treatment of stakeholders and shareholders by the management of a company to prevent the conflicts regarding their interests . similarly the word transparency can be defined as or can be expressed as providing all the non-financial information and financial material within a durable time and at low rate cost so that it could be reliable , accurate and should be valid for the decision making process of a company. Responsibility word can be related with the compliance of all the rules and regulations which were drafted under the articles and are in the audit process and operations. On the other hand we can define the word accountability as laying down the powers of boards so that the board of directors could answer to the shareholders and stakeholders as regarding a corporate entity .Hence, to establish the corporate governance framework, various corporations such as organization for economic cooperation and development and global corporate governance forum, world bank had been assigned the task to discuss the issue regarding corporate governance. Thus, a huge number of countries in the developing and developed economy are still in the process for the reconstruction of their legislation and also reviewing them and even some of them came out of whole new law, rules and regulations.

A corporation is basically known to be various combinations of stakeholders and shareholders named as employees, customers, directors, vendor partners, society, government and investors. In such kind of situation and in the changing scenario, a corporation should be just and equitable to its shareholders in all the transactions. This is becoming very important in today's pace of globalization where organizations need to capture and preserve the best human capital and even to access the global pools of capital market. Unless and until any organization demonstrates and embraces such kind of ethical conduct, it will not be able to get success in future. Corporations also needs to acknowledge the it's growth, and such cooperation will be enhanced by the adherence of the best governance practices.

Thus, management is required to act as trustees of the shareholders and prevent the asymmetry assistance between various sections, especially between the owner - managers and the rest of the shareholders. Effective corporate governance structure needs to be flexible according to market dynamics, so that it responds and yet it should be unwavering regarding its values and ethics.

FACTORS AFFECTING THE QUALITY OF CORPORATE GOVERNENCE

Corporate governance is an essential factor which influences the long term economic health of the companies and it resides only in the part of larger economic context in which organizations operates. The structure depends upon the regulatory and intuitional environment, legal, awareness and business ethics of the environmental and societal interests of the constituents in which they operates. The quality of corporate governance mainly depends upon the factors mentioned below:-

1. Ability of the Board
2. Adequacy of the process
3. Integrity of the management
4. Standard of corporate reporting
5. Involvement of shareholders in the management
6. Commitment level of individual board members

If organizations requires full benefits of the global capital market , benefit by the economies of scale , capture efficiency gains and attract long term capital the assumption of the corporate governance standards must be consistent , credible , inspiring and coherent . The amount to which organizations should observe the basic proposition of a good corporate governance is very important factor for taking the major investment decisions. The global flow of capital helps to enable companies in seeking financial help from the larger and bigger pool of investors.

RELATIONSHIP BETWEEN INDIA AND THE SCENARIO OF CORPORATE GOVERNANCE

In 1991, India eventually established its progress in the direction of welcoming and open economy. Presently the role of corporate governance has very essential significance towards the economic condition of our country. From the time of 1991 onwards it was seen that there was a great trend in the dimension of the stock exchange i.e., aggregate of registered firms was intensifying consistently. It tends to emphasize more focus on transparency and shareholders value expansion because if India draws more nations for foreign direct investment, then they have to pay more focus towards it.

The concept of corporate governance in India established until 1991, only after the period when liberalization takes place. India was lagging behind. The most important startup was taken by India to improve the securities and exchange board of India in 1992. Earlier the main motive of the SEBI was to oversee and systematize stock exchange, but slowly and slowly many regulations was formed by it. The next big change happened in India was the creation of confederation of Indian industry (CII) in 1996 .which helps initially to evolve the set of certain laws rules and regulations towards corporate governance as to begin the act towards it for the Indian companies . Then afterwards clause 49 came into existence as a part of agreement for the companies listed on Indian stock exchange because of the two main leading groups Kumar mangalam Birla and Narayan murthy. As these two committees starts putting the best work practices on corporate governance. However clause 49 was forced to be amended due to some scandals done by the companies like Enron, Satyam, and World com etc. And to overcome the issues that was happened to these organizations to fall down and shatter the economies of their nation.

Clause 49 of the Indian stock exchange agreement came into existence from 2000 to 2003 .it accommodates all the set of laws , rules and regulations and even the requirements of minimum and maximum numbers of liberated directors , different necessary committees , audit committee rules , board members , and limits etc. . Those firms who were not adapting these principles mentioned in clause 49 were given financial penalties and were removed from the list.

We can differentiate here the clause 49 and sarbens –oxley act of 2002. The sarbens – oxley act of 2002 was came into existence for the corporations or companies that are listed in the US stock exchange. Clause 49 was primarily based on the concept of sarbens- oxley act of 2002. When it comes to the point of number of directors and responsibilities of management they both are similar to each other. They even also depict the same rule for the refusal of loan to directors, regarding insider trading and etc. The main and the basic difference between the two is mainly in the sarbens –oxeyl law. If fraud or any such kind of activity takes place then the person could be charges up to 20 years of imprisonment, but when it comes to clause 49 it basically lacks in the matter. There is no such legislation and condition for it but in case of clause 49 the SEBI has a right to file a criminal proceeding or punishment for not following the rules and not agreeing with clause 49 exhibits the company with the list.

Corporate governance paid emphasis not only on corporations but also to the countries in various ways as well. Unemployment can also be reduced by this as it attracts more and more firms and also directs to growth. Wealth can be generated by adapting good management practices and by much better distribution of resources. This is because of the better operational performances. By the adaption of better corporate governance it also helps in the reduction of financial crisis. As these financial crises would have been very adverse effects on the company's economy. If the corporate governance practices are performed properly, then this will also help to create better links with the respective stakeholders and shareholders.

Corporate governance has become a major problem for all the countries around the world due to the fraudulent behavior of the corporations that had caused countries to go through the financial crisis. The pattern of following this structure is more or less the same. As we can compare also starting from the Satyam computers limited of India to Enron of the US. Failure in the performance of companies in a big amount has created a havoc in the corporate industry and also have cause the economic meltdown in ours. The Indian government felt to promote good corporate governance practices amongst the country as an intermediate action to reveal the scandals. Else for the executives of foreign multinational companies understanding corporate governance issues was also very important to execute their business and trading with India.

CHAPTER TWENTY-THREE

INDIA'S UNEMPLOYMENT

Author: Nipun, B.B.A.,LL.B from Geeta Institute of law.

Co-author: Mayank, B.B.A.,LL.B from Geeta Institute of law.

India is the world's sixth most populous country. With a population of almost 135 million people and the world's youngest population. The majority of the population is between the ages of 18 and 35, however despite this, India continues to struggle with unemployment. In their own country, Indians are unable to find work. There is no job for the youth, thus they are free.

India is a country in the process of evolving. It indicates that the country is on the edge of being developed. India, like other developing countries, is grappling with a slew of social, economic, and political issues. Any developed country should be the one that succeeds in overcoming challenges and issues.

Unemployment occurs when a person is willing and able to work for a certain pay or salary but is unable to do so.

Unemployment has been a big issue in India since the country's inception. Despite our government's best efforts, we have been unable to resolve this issue.

Reasons

1. The population is large. Being the world's second most populated country. India has a limited amount of resources. India's population is growing at such a rapid pace that it will overtake China as the world's most populous country in the coming years.

2. Low educational level- Even though the level of education is not very high, the people of are not well educated.

3. Lack of initiative- The Indian people do not take initiative on their own. They rely on the government for job and career opportunities. India's

people aspire to go forward from where they are now.

The country's crime rate is rising as a result of high unemployment. Because of unemployment, robbery, rape, and murder cases are on the rise. Our country's youth are diverted from its intended path. There is an old proverb that says, "The devil's house is an empty mind." This is ideal in this circumstance.

These are some of the statistics that reflect India's unemployment rate. The unemployment rate in India reached a new high of 7.91 percent in December, up from 7% and 7.75 percent in November and October, respectively.

According to the NSSO Survey, the unemployment rate was 2.2 percent in 2011-12. Males aged 15 to 29 years old in rural areas increased from 5% in 2011-12 to 17.4% in 2017-18. Females in rural areas increased from 4.8 percent to 13.6 percent. Urban youngsters had a higher unemployment rate than their rural counterparts (18.7 percent for males and 27.2 percent for females).

Unemployment is mostly a financial problem. As a result, it is critical that the country's economic policy be revised. In our country, there is no shortage of labour. Cottage and small-scale industries should provide employment opportunities for them. Aside from that, family planning must be prioritized. Every effort must be made to slow the rate of population growth. This will be quite beneficial in resolving this issue.

The unemployment rate grew from 5.55 percent in 1991 to 7.91 percent in 2020, according to the data, with an annual change of 0.06 percent in 1991 and 1.84 percent in 2020. With 34 percent of the population unemployed, Haryana ranks first. India is ranked 85th in the world when it comes to unemployment.

Haryana 34.1 percent, Rajasthan 27 percent, Jharkhand 17.3 percent, Jammu and Kashmir 15 percent, Tripura 14.2 percent, Bihar 16 percent, and India's capital city Delhi 9.8 percent are among the states with the highest unemployment rates.

<u>The government employs the following strategies to reduce unemployment</u>

1. Use of labor-intensive technology: Because India has the world's largest workforce, the government is focusing on the use of labour in industries rather than machines.

2. Increasing Agriculture Investment- The majority of our population is dependent on and involved in agriculture. As a result, the government is investing heavily in agriculture in order for it to be exploited as a business by the people.

3. Agriculture diversification—In India, rice and wheat are the most common crops, but farmers are free during the off-season. As a result, the government is educating people on how to raise crops during this time.

4. Labour-intensive industrial growth- In order to address the urban unemployment problem, the organised industrial sector must absorb a sufficient number of workers. The usage of capital-intensive technologies imported from overseas is to blame for the organised industrial sector's failure to produce enough employment possibilities.

Unemployment among educated young people is a big issue. There are dozens of candidates for each vacancy. Only a few candidates are hired out of the hundreds who are interviewed. A student devotes several years of his or her life to his or her studies. Even after receiving a Bachelor's or Master's degree, India's youth is battling unemployment.

Finally, I hope that the effects of Corona will be removed from the country and the world as soon as possible, and that people will be able to find work. I also sincerely implore that the government, rather than ignoring the issue of unemployment, pay greater attention to it. India's people and administration are taking the required efforts to address the country's unemployment problem.

CHAPTER TWENTY-FOUR

HUMAN RIGHTS VIOLATION IN DEMOCRATIC REPUBLIC OF CONGO

<u>**Author**</u>: Aman Tiwari, IV year of B.A.,LL.B from Delhi Metropolitan Education Noida, affiliated to Guru Gobind Singh Indraprastha University Delhi.

<u>INTRODUCTION</u>

"The Democratic Republic of the Congo" is a powerful country with a strong central government. The president along with the lower house of the Parliament are elected by people (National Assembly). In the month of December on 30th during the year 2018, presidential, parliamentary, and provincial are the three elections which were conducted after a two-year hiatus.

Felix Tshisekedi was proclaimed the victor during 2018 presidential election by the "National Independent Electoral Commission" on January 10, 2019. The 2018 election was marked by irregularities, which were condemned by several spectators.

Congolese National Police, is in charge of law enforcement and public order. The National Intelligence Agency, which is controlled by the president, is in charge of both internal and foreign intelligence. The Ministry of Defense oversees the "Armed Forces of the Democratic Republic of the Congo", as well as the intelligence service provided by the military. They are primarily responsible for foreign security, although they are virtually entirely focused on domestic security. The Republican Guard is overseen by the presidency, while the Directorate General for Migration is overseen by the Ministry of Interior. Congolese National Police along with the Directorate General for Migration, is in charge of border control. The authorities which look after the civilians didn't have the power over security personnel. Numerous violations were committed by members who were in the security forces.

"Unlawful or arbitrary killings, including extrajudicial killings; forced disappearances; torture and cases of cruel, inhuman, or degrading treatment or punishment; harsh and life-threatening prison conditions; arbitrary detention; political prisoners or detainees; serious problems with the judiciary's independence; arbitrary or unlawful invasion of privacy; serious abuses in an internal conflict, including the killing of civilians. Severe restrictions on free expression and the press, including violence, threats of violence, or unjustified arrests of journalists, censorship, and criminal libel; interference with the rights to peaceful assembly and freedom of association; serious acts of official corruption; lack of investigation and accountability for violence against women; trafficking in persons; crimes involving violence or threats of violence targeting persons with disabilities, members of national minorities, and members of national minorities."

Although numerous human rights violations went unpunished, the government took certain measures to spot, probe, take legal action, and penalize bureaucrats who executed them. Authorities, particularly at higher levels, frequently failed to investigate, convict, or punish individuals who were guilty. Some government officials were convicted of unlawful death, sexual assault, cruelty, arbitrary imprisonment, and bribery, while law enforcement officers who executed atrocities were occasionally punished.

In Kasai area and particularly in restive eastern region illegal armed groups and government security personal continued to abuse their power over people. Torture, unlawful killings, damage to government, personal estate, disappearances and gender-based violence were among the violations. Child soldiers and forced labour were also recruited, abducted, and held by illegal armed organizations. Military action was taken against certain unlawful armed organizations, and some armed group members were investigated and punished for human rights violations.

As a result of COVID-19 limitations, poor households experienced greater food insecurity, while jails were persistently overcrowded. Armed conflicts and intercommunal violence persisted in certain regions, killing hundreds and displacing hundreds of thousands of people. For egregious human rights abuses like as extrajudicial murders and summary executions, government troops and armed groups have continued to enjoy impunity. Sexual violence against women has escalated as a result of the conflict. The administration continues to stifle "Freedom of speech and the press". Journalists have been imprisoned, and human rights activists have been threatened with death and prosecuted.

BACKGROUND

The situation with regards to constitutional rights persisted severe, along with conflicts happening in the ruling coalition. A surge of hostility, mainly in several parts of the country, consisting of armed groups along with neighboring countries, has intensified the humanitarian situation. In provinces of South Kivu, North Kivu, Tanganyika and Ituri thousands of armed group soldiers surrendered themselves early this year. The government's attention was diverted away from disarmament, demobilization, and reintegration programmes as a result of its concentration on COVID-19 and other illnesses.

The President announced steps to combat the COVID-19 epidemic on March 18th, including travel limitations, closing of borders, and disallowing of gatherings of more than 20 individuals. The President declared a state of emergency for 30 days on March 24, which was prolonged till 23rd of April and approved by the Parliament and the Court. It was lifted on 22nd of July, following a slowing in COVID-19 deaths and cases in late June, and limitations were gradually eased.

New appointments to the army and the court have been made, but neither institution's behavior changed much, creating a serious barrier to human rights protection.

On November 23, a military court in North Kivu condemned military leader "Ntabo Ntaberi alias Sheka", the commander of "Nduma Defense of Congo", and sentenced him for life imprisonment for committing severe offence against the general public perpetrated in North Kivu in the year 2007 till 2017. 400 men, women and children were charged with rape in the year 2010. A representative of Rwanda's Democratic Forces for Liberation was also given the death penalty. After a two-year trial in which 178 victims took part, two Sheka accomplices were penalized for 15 years in jail.

<u>COVID-19</u>

As of November 7, 2020, doctors of Congolese have documented more than over 11,500 Corona virus infections in 22 regions, with 315 deaths. Given the restricted testing capability, the number of instances is likely to be greater. State emergency was declared at Congolese during the period of March 24th till August 15th in order to stop the virus from spreading. The Schools, bars, and worship place along with restaurants were shut down, as were borders, big gatherings, and schools, restaurants, and bars. Around 19 million students were impacted by school closures. On March 30, police opened fire at the people of "Bundu dia Kongo politico-religious organization" which was involved at marching in Kinshasa to "chase the spirit of the coronavirus," according to a UN source. At least three people were killed, and 11 others were injured. Because to Covid-19 travel limitations, the government also ordered the mining companies to halt limiting personnel on the job on July 14.

<u>RIGHT TO HEALTH</u>

The virus imposed severe burden on the health system that was already underfunded and overburdened, as well as poorly compensated health personnel who were simultaneously dealing with other outbreaks of diseases.

The government of United States supplied fifty oxygen support systems to the government of the DRC to aid in the fight against the outbreak. The number of confirmed COVID-19 cases and fatalities had grown at the end. During the mid-year, virus rate had dropped. In 2018 tenth Ebola pandemic began and had killed at least 2,287 and infected at least 3,470 individuals, while 6,000 peoples were killed during measles outbreak.

<u>RIGHT TO EDUCATION</u>

The administration shuttered schools, colleges, in the month of March 19, affecting around 27 million pupils. Many children were exposed to the possibility of being recruited into military organizations, as well as can be the victim of sexual assault, child marriage, and child labor, as a result of school closures. On August 10th, schools reopened.

Thousands of children's educations have been disrupted as a result of armed wars.

RIGHTS: ECONOMIC, SOCIAL AND CULTURAL

Low-income households were harmed by COVID-19-related lockdowns and other limitations, while the government took steps to ameliorate the situation by providing vital services including electricity & water. Houses in rural and urban areas, as well as those in border regions, lost major sources of income as necessity for sector employees and those engaged in cross border commerce fell.

In mining business, enforcement of environmental and labor regulations has been failed which was done by the government, exposing many employees to hazardous substances and causing birth abnormalities in the children. Without basic equipment such as face mask and gloves, women, men and children are working in certain mines. They also had lung infections and urinary tract infections, among other health issues. Child labour was often used, as they were forced to do mining operations, no transparency was awarded in mining rights, bribery and tariff fraud.

DISAPPROPRIATE USE OF FORCE

Pandemic prohibit people to gather together, security officers used excessive force to disperse peaceful protests. Protests erupted in a number of areas on July 9 in response to the selection of President of Electoral Commission. In reaction to the mainly peaceful protests, police used disproportionate power, resulting in death of one demonstrator. A lot more people were harmed due to the incident.

FORCE USED BY GOVERNMENT AND ARMED GROUP FOR ATTACKING ON CIVILIANS

According to "United Nations High Commissioner for Human Rights," around 13,00 people were killed by the armed groups of the non-state including the government troops between October 2019 and June 2020. Along with this, more than hundred people were slaughtered during the middle of the year.

"More than 130 armed groups attacked citizens in the eastern Congo districts of North Kivu, South Kivu, and Ituri. Among the militia associations were the mainly ethnic Lendu Cooperative for the Development of Congo (CODECO), the largely Ugandan Allied Democratic Forces (ADF), the Nduma Defense of Congo-Renové (NDC-R), the largely Rwandan Democratic Forces for the Liberation of Rwanda (FDLR) and allied Congolese Nyatura groups, the Mazembe and Yakutumba Mai Mai militia groups, and several Burundian armed groups. Many of its leaders have been charged with war crimes such as ethnic cleansing, rape, forced child recruitment, and pillaging."

Due to tension in the regions of South Kivu's, many people were murdered between the month of February 2019 to June 2020.

UNLAWFUL KILLINGS

There have been several claims that the government or its agents have killed people in an arbitrary or criminal manner. The Military tribunals helped to determine the killings done by the security force and also the killings were admissible and also prosecuted those who were.

Hundreds of people have died due to armed warfare in regions of South Kivu, North Kivu, and Ituri. Millions of people were forced to evacuate their places as a result of armed group attacks. According to the UNJHRO, militants of armed factions conducted killings in middle of the year, killing individuals, women as well as children.

"The Allied Democratic Forces (ADF)", military organization running operation in the "Democratic Republic of Congo and Uganda", was responsible for a spike in violence year after authorities conducted preventative assaults against the group. The ADF massacred many civilians in territory of Irumu, on May 25 and 26. They are also suspected of killing seven civilians on August 15 and 58 persons in raids in the region.

Meanwhile, in the middle of the year, troops were accused of murdering 14 people and wounding 49 others. They also detained and arrested 297 people without cause.

In the month of March and June, provoked militia strikes in Ituri murdered hundreds of civilians and displaced over 200,000 people. The majority of the killings were committed by Lendu militants, while most of the victims were from Hema and residents of Alur.

In Ituri, allegations of inter-communal confrontations began between the Alur and Hema groups in May and June. At least 100 individuals were killed in Tanganyika province during clashes between the Twa and Bantu populations.

BRUTALITY FACED BY GIRLS AND WOMEN

Sexual exploitations of girls and women has risen, notably due to the conflict in eastern area. Groups attacked women and men along with children and 97 incidents have been recorded by the UNJHRO in May up from 53 in April. While armed organizations were the major perpetrators, there was an increase in sexual assault which were reported between April and May by state security forces.

EXTRAJUDICIAL EXECUTIONS

Across the country, extrajudicial executions were still common. Military organizations were accountable for the bulk of the killings, agents working for the state were also involved, especially in conflict-affected regions. According to the UNJHRO, agents were responsible for killing couple of hundred individuals in the first half of the year, including 33 women and 18 children.

There were at least 55 extrajudicial murders by security personnel in July alone, with about 11 of them being women and two children. Armed organizations killed 248 individuals in the same time period, including 34 women and 11 children. For these and other human rights breaches and atrocities, state authorities and armed group combatants were seldom convicted. Lack of resources and judicial independence remained significant impediments to achieving accountability.

FREEDOM OF EXPRESSION

Members working for the media were bullied by the authorities. They accused journalists and news organizations of upsetting the public order and violating professional ethics. Several journalists have been detained on false charges.

Hundreds of people have been harassed and intimidated as a result of their criticism of government policy, especially on social media. They were attacked, imprisoned, and convicted in certain circumstances. Authorities have intimidated and harassed journalists around the country, and the government has ordered the shutdown of specific television programmes or outlets. During the time of state emergency in order to prevent the spread of virus the security used force against the protesters.

"Dek'son Assani Kamango, Journalist of Radio Omega", was detained on 7 February on charges of "insulting the Maniema provincial administration." "Christine Tshibuyi, a Kinshasa-based reporter", got threat calls on May 9 when he published a piece on attacks on journalists in Kasai Oriental province's Mbuji-Mayi town. A four-wheel-drive vehicle identical to the Guard of Republican smashed into the car on the same day, leading her to crash into a wall. A guy smacked her across the face, causing her to bleed. He was accompanied by four security officials. She stated that she reported the event to authorities, but that no inquiry was conducted.

Both state officials and armed organizations have threatened, intimidated, arrested, and detained human rights advocates. Dr. Denis Mukwege, a Nobel Laureate, has received death threats as a result of his support for severe criminal punishment.

The administration of Mongala withdrew the credentials of 13 journalists on June 17, five radio stations were ordered to be temporary closed and halted the transmission of various political television and radio programmes.

INTERNATIONAL JUSTICE

Although international community along with the government took steps to prevent it, the judicial system of Congolese didn't stop prosecuting war criminals. While tens of thousands of offenders have perpetrated heinous crimes in the DRC, just 12 prosecutions who committed the crimes have been held in military courts.

"Luis Moreno-Ocampo, the Chief Prosecutor of the International Criminal Court (ICC), said in 2004 that he had decided to begin an investigation into crimes allegedly executed in the DRC since the Rome Statute of the ICC took effect on July 1, 2002. Thomas Lubanga Dyilo, Germain Katanga, Mathieu Ngudjolo Chui, and, most recently, Callixte Mbarushimana have all been apprehended, but Bosco Ntaganda is still on the loose".

Children who are under the age of 15 years are being enlisted and conscripted and used by Lubanga Dyilo to actively participate in hostilities is still in trial at the International Criminal Court (ICC). Katanga along with Ngudjolo Chui were charged for various heinous crimes against the individuals, and for promoting child labor before the International Criminal Court.

INDIGENOUS PEOPLES

When the Indigenous Twa people were forcibly evacuated from the "Kahuzi Biega National Park", authorities failed to uphold their commitments. The community has been evacuated in waves since 1975, despite promises of comparable replacement land, educational and job opportunities, health facilities, and the release of community members imprisoned for invading the Park. Meanwhile, the discussions which were going on between Park authorities and representatives of Twa for over different land for the town have come to a halt.

Twa men and women were held responsible of unlawful actions in the Park in February, including key negotiator Chief Jean-Marie Kasula. Their trial in front of the tribunal was not a fair trial and hence they were prosecuted for 15 years' imprisonment. In August, 4 out of 8 were freed on bond from jail. During the year end, their convictions had not been overturned on appeal.

<u>UNJHRO'S STRUCTURE</u>

The UNJHRO is divided into various specialized sections:

- "The Transitional Justice and Fight Against Impunity Unit" is in charge of supervising the administration of justice and prosecuting those who commit grave human rights abuses.
- The division of "Training, Institution Building, and Awareness (TIBA)" assists society organizations in filing complaints and requests with government agencies in response to human rights abuses.
- In collaboration with the Field Offices, the Reporting and Investigations Unit conducts in-depth investigations of significant human rights abuses, particularly in remote parts of the DRC. It also manages a human rights database and is in charge of data gathering and analysis, report preparation, and database administration.
- "The Strategic Planning and Project Support Unit" ensures that the UNJHRO's planning is carried out in accordance with its priorities. It also helps the UNJHRO with its programmes and operations.
- Under immediate threat, the Protection Unit seeks to protect the people from different backgrounds. Also the Protection Funds are managed by the Protection Unit.

<u>UNJHRO'S MANDATE</u>

"The United Nations Joint Human Rights Office (UNJHRO) was established in February 2008 by the MONUSCO Human Rights Division (HRD) and the former Office of the UN High Commissioner for Human Rights in the Democratic Republic of the Congo (OHCHR/DRC)." The two offices have been fully integrated, and the UNJHRO currently fulfils its respective mandates. "The United Nations Security Council (Resolutions 1756 of 15 May 2007, 1794 of 21 December 2007, and 1856 of 22 December 2008)" mandated the "MONUSCO Human Rights Division (HRD)" so that more protection and promotion can be provided to the humans, majorly to the children, women and also the vulnerable groups. It also focused to keep a check on violations done so that it can be stopped and justice can prevail leading to development and implementation of strategy.

"The OHCHR/DRC was established in 1996 by an agreement between the UN High Commissioner for Human Rights and the Government of the Democratic Republic of the Congo (DRC) to monitor the country's human rights situation, present reports on human rights violations requiring urgent intervention by any of the thematic Independent Experts, and strengthen national institutions (both governmental and non-governmental) working on human rights issues to ensure that the DRC increases its human rights protection."

On December 23, 2009, the United Nations Security Council overwhelmingly approved "Resolution 1906 (2009)," and also extended the mission of MONUC till 31 May, 2010. The resolution came to the conclusion that long term peace in the country is not possible until state security forces strengthen their respect for human rights. Because almost every word of the resolution references human rights, it offers up potential for improving the respect in the country for human rights and also puts pressure on UNHJRO to help the government and MONUC to reach the mandate.

<u>**ASSISTING ON POSITIVE CHANGE**</u>

To battle five of the most pervasive and the most serious human rights abuses in country, the UNJHRO launched a new work approach during 2009. Five Task Forces (TFs) was formed as an outcome of this new approach and each one concentrating on one of the five main areas outlined below: Violations of economic rights/illegal mining; arbitrary arrests and unlawful detentions and disappearances; discrimination of sex; arbitrary executions; Torture leading to deaths in imprisonment.

The UNJHRO's day-to-day operations are organized under these Task Forces. Task Force is made up of members from specialized groups who work together to devise plans to increase the level of constitutional rights.

In order to promote foreign community initiatives implemented in the provinces, worldwide strategy to help sufferers and the people who have faced violence is developed which includes:

- Torture victims Funds;
- Justice Provided to the Victims of Sexual Violence;
- Protection Funds for the Victims, along with the witnesses and the defenders of human rights.

APPROACH

The main principle was to provide steps to the civilians in the country encouraging them to report the breaches of human rights to the concerned authorities which will eventually help to strengthen ability of government to help the civilians. This can be achieved by helping the citizen know about their rights, providing space for their complaints, giving power to the civil society to educate civilians about human rights, adopting strategies that will enhance the awareness about rights and obligation of the people and also promoting government's power to fix the issues and encouraging to take actions.

The everyday activities involve the reporting of violations caused to the humans and then assisting to use the remedies. In order to combat impunity, the UNJHRO collaborates with government in order to improve the overall situation by enacting policies that help to achieve the International Norms. The UNJHRO's methodology was based on former similar project best practices, as well as strategies and work plans developed by the "UNJHRO's Task Forces, Units, and Field Teams."

HUMAN RIGHTS VIOLATION AND HOW IT COMBAT TO GIVE JUSTICE

Through a wide network of collaborators, the Officers collect data on accusations of Constitutional rights breaches and by correlating information obtained during field operations, the Officers authenticate claims and comment on Constitutional rights breaches. To counteract threats, the UNJHRO has established procedures to safeguard victims and witnesses in collaboration with its network of non-governmental organisations (NGOs).

The UNJHRO concentrates on situations that are outside the scope of other actors' capabilities. Cases which were presented before the court, and the status of every case is kept track of. UNJHRO also works to ensure that criminal procedure is followed and that detention facility conditions are improved.

HOW THE STATE PREVENTED HUMAN RIGHT VIOLATIONS?

The UNJHRO provided judicial authorities and partners for prosecuting the cases logically and technically. Financial assistance was also offered in order to improve the countrywide access to Justice Program. Furthermore, the UNJHRO also works with institutions and the state, to enhance their capacity to hear citizen complaints through the parliamentary network for human rights. "The Protection Unit" helps to provide safety to the individuals belonging to different background.

CONCLUSION

It is clearly evident that the country faced a lot of violations and conflicts that were done by the armed troops which influenced the major situation throughout the period. The forces in the country influenced the people and led to a lot of violation in the western portion of the country. The basic rights under the constitution was not provided to the humans and they were treated dreadfully. Excessive force was used by the agents leading to death of the civilians. Women, Children and everyone around the country was brutality harassed and was not provided the basic living.

CHAPTER TWENTY-FIVE

LEGISLATIVE REVIEW ON LABOUR WAGE CODE

Author: Aman Tiwari, IV year of B.A.,LL.B from Delhi Metropolitan Education Noida, affiliated to Guru Gobind Singh Indraprastha University Delhi.

INTRODUCTION

The Wage Code Bill, 2019, is a comprehensive legislation that unifies and improves numerous labour regulations by combining four of them with regard to wages, bonus payments, and related concerns. It is the first of the four labour codes to be granted Act status: The Code on Wages 2019, the

Code on Occupational Safety, Health, and Working Conditions 2019, the Code on Social Security 2019, and the Code on Industrial Relations 2019.

As previously stated, the Wage Code Bill, 2019 consolidated and simplified four statutes: the Minimum Wage Act of 1948(for establishing minimum pay rates in particular occupations), the Payment of Wages Act of 1936 (to govern the payment of salaries to specific types of employees), the Payment of Bonus Act of 1965 (for the payment of bonuses to employees in particular enterprises based on earnings, production, or productivity), and the Equal Remuneration Act of 1976 (to provide equal pay for men and women and to eliminate gender discrimination in the workplace).

This bill consolidates, streamlines, and rationalises current labour laws for ease of doing business, eliminates outdated laws, gives unique definitions, has universal application across India to all establishments, employees, and employers, eliminates social, gender, and income inequities, and intends to create uniformity through the establishment of a National Floor Wage.

According to Shri Santosh Kumar Gangwar, Minister of State (I/C) for Labour and Employment, it is a historic Bill that aspires to reform outdated and antiquated labour rules into more responsible and transparent ones that are urgently needed. There are now 17 labour laws that are more than 50 years old, with some dating back to the pre-independence era.

<u>BACKGROUND</u>

According to a survey of the references, there are more than 40 Central Labour Laws, some of which have become outdated or ineffective in resolving grievances or irregularities. In 2015, the Indian government announced plans to merge 40 Central Labour Laws into four codes in order to address gaps and inconsistencies in present laws by creating new ones that are more suited to today's demands and pay policies.

The Wage Code Law was introduced in the Lok Sabha for the first time in August 2017 and referred to the Parliamentary Standing Committee, which issued a report in December 2018 with 24 suggestions, 17 of which were adopted into the bill. Due to the general elections, the bill expired. The bill was reintroduced in 2019 and approved in both chambers. On July 30, 2019, the bill was passed in the Lok Sabha, and on August 2, 2019, it was passed in the Rajya Sabha. On August 8, 2019, India's President, Ram Nath Kovind, granted his approval to the bill. As a result, it was given the name Wage Code Bill, 2019. On July 7, 2020, the proposed regulations under the Code ("Rules") were made available in the form of a handbook for comment and suggestions. The Wage Code Bill of 2019 is set to go into effect on April 1, 2021.

SCOPE OF THE BILL

Because of its coverage and beneficial ramifications, the bill has a broad scope. The Wage Code Bill, 2019, consists of IX Chapters and 69 Clauses that aim to simplify, consolidate, and rationalise current Labour Laws.

- Definitions are provided in Chapter I and are relevant throughout the code.
- Chapter II-IV includes provisions relating to the Wage Payment, Bonus Payment, Equal Remuneration Provision, and Minimum Payment.
- The regulations pertaining to the Central Advisory Board and State Advisory Boards, Payment of Dues, Claims and Audits, Inspector-cum-Facilitator, and Offenses and Penalties are covered in Chapters V-VIII.
- Miscellaneous Provisions are covered in Chapter IX.
- The bill is expected to benefit around 500 million employees across the country. It will apply to firms, workers, and employers in all Indian states and union territories.
- "The wage code, clearly states the objective to promote equity and labour welfare on the one hand and encourage investment and setting up of more enterprises on the other, thereby catalysing creation of more employment opportunities."
- It also includes salary choices made by the Central Government for jobs like as railways, mining, and oil fields.

CRUX OF THE BILL

It is comprehensive, simple to follow, and is adopted by employers and businesses. It has both good and bad aspects.

- It provides for the standardisation of salaries and bonus payments in all areas of work, including organised and unorganised sectors, as well as commercial establishments, and makes compliance simpler.
- It defines and regulates the terms employee, pay, worker, contractor, and contract labour.
- To determine minimum pay, it takes into account schedule and income levels, as well as talent and geographical area.
- "It is consistent with the Equal Remuneration Act, the Code, inter-alia, includes provisions prohibiting discrimination on grounds of gender

(i) with respect to wages by employers, with respect to same work or work of a similar nature done by employees and (ii) with respect to recruitment of employees for same work or work of a similar nature."

- It aims a consistent floor pay that applies to all sorts of establishments and trades, with the exception of hazardous industries, which have their own minimum pay.
- Minimum salaries are subject to revision/review every five years at the most.

POSITIVE IMPICATIONS OF THE BILL

- It protects disadvantaged employees and promotes fair competition by extending the legal protections provided by the minimum wage and floor wage to all wage earners across the country, regardless of schedule or pay limitation. Millions of India's low wage employees will benefit as a result of this.
- It advocates central government fixing of minimum pay across the country based on standard of life, with state governments required to establish minimum pay equal to or higher than the floor pay. As a result, the wage-setting process will alter, wages will rise, and income disparities within and between states will be reduced.
- It simplifies and rationalises India's complex minimum wage system while also allowing employees and corporations to engage in collective bargaining.
- Through an equal payment and compensation clause, it removes gender discrepancies in compensation and covers transgender persons in its scope.
- It requests more overtime compensation, a larger gratuity, and post-retirement benefits.
- It raises the limitation period from two to three years, giving workers more time to submit claims.
- It introduces compoundable offences, allowing for settlement and dismissal of charges between employer and employee.

NEGATIVE IMPLICATIONS OF THE BILL

- The code requires greater wages, which may hinder businesses from hiring.

- The government's involvement to establish a minimum wage will disrupt wage equilibrium.
- Reduced take-home pay as a result of increasing PF (provident fund) deductions from net pay.
- Increased socioeconomic inequity as a result of imposing minimum wages depending on geography, which might lead to industry outsourcing jobs.
- Lack of consistency and compliance as a result of states' ability to set bonus ceilings, which makes employees in some areas ineligible for wage bonuses.
- Due to its calculation based on the inclusion of allowance in the basic salary, the company's gratuity expense rises.
- It has precedents and is at odds with other present labour laws.

<u>CONCLUSION</u>

The 2019 Wage Code Bill is a friendly legislation. Its goal is to reform outdated and antiquated labour regulations, as well as to improve openness and accountability in their implementation. The 2019 Wage Code Bill significantly aligns companies' and employees' interests. It will bring major changes to India's pay system, as well as subsume four central laws and uphold 40 others.

The bill applies the minimum wage to all employees, regardless of their schedule or income group. It also streamlines the country's minimum wage system. The law is a step forward in meeting long-standing labour union objectives. The Wage Code Bill of 2019, on the other hand, includes several loose ends and fails to address several critical concerns.

It emphasises the minimum wage but says nothing about equitable wages. Despite the fact that the code was reviewed in detail by multiple individuals, no representative from the labour union was present. The Code, like all other current central labour legislation, fails to protect migratory workers.

In addition, the code permits web-based inspection, which is in violation of one of the ILO's requirements. It fails to impose sufficient fines/penalties on violators. The code's provision benefits the business community, but it falls short of improving the lives of millions of low wage workers in India. In a nutshell, the law is a blanket policy with far-reaching positive implications.

<u>Author's Biography</u>

Penultimate Law Student passionate about enhancing knowledge at every step of life and a keen learner with an aim to expertise at everything.

CHAPTER TWENTY-SIX

NEED FOR SPEAKING ORDERS OR REASONED DECISIONS

Author: Ananaya Chauhan, IV year of B.A.,LL.B from Delhi Metropolitan Education, Noida Affiliated To Guru Gobind Singh Indraprastha University, Delhi.

Equity is the basis of the law that we regard as "reasonableness." Justice makes sure that the law is reasonable as it will apply equally without any differences to everyone. Justice also helps to provide the required punishment or relief to the person concerned according to his conduct. Justice is an important element which is required to be followed by everyone in order to achieve equality, fairness, and equity. Justice is the basic requirement of each member of the society, even in the preamble of the Constitution of India Justice has been given the first priority in order to provide social, economic and political justice to every persons of the society. It is related to the value and morals of the people and also their behavior towards the society, it helps to provide for the balance in the society.

Natural justice, as the name suggests is being originated by the nature and is also regarded as the "law of nature". In the natural sense it talks about what is right and what is wrong, it adheres to the basic principles of the nature which are not man made and cannot be changed according to the view of man. It aims to provide fairness to the persons and also to secure justice to the persons. After a many hundred years, finally there was these following

"Principles of Natural Justice (PNJ)":

1. "Nemo in propria causa judex, esse debet" - It stands for "Rule against Bias" which states that "no one can be made a judge in its own cause", basically it says that the judge has no right to be impartial with anyone and has to give the judgement according to the facts of the case and it should be justified. There should not be any type of bias by the judge for his own benefit.
2. "Audi alteram partem" - It stands for "Rule of fair hearing" which means that "every person has the right to be heard in the court". He has the right to defend himself and give his statement and he should not be unheard in the court. It is duty of the judge to act fairly and listen to both the side of parties.

Other than the two above mentioned principles, according to the recent trends a new dimension has been added to the principles of natural justice for a better and enhanced law system which is knowns as the "Duty to pass the speaking orders".

<u>**SPEAKING ORDERS OR REASONED DECISIONS MEANING**</u>

As the name already suggests, the meaning of this principle if that the order given by the judges must speak for itself herby meaning that it must have a reason for giving such decision and also the person has the right to know about such reason and also result of the inquiry. It refers to an order which already speaks for itself by giving the proper reasons for the same. It is important so that it can be effective in order to obtain judicial review. It follows a very basic rule that must be known to everyone that, justice must not only be done, but it must also appear to be done. It also helps to have faith in the authorities that the decision provided by them are correct and in good conscience. The reasons which are to provided, should not only be "rubber-stamp" reasons but also particularized, understandable and clear explanation which has connection among the case and its facts along with the conclusion it is based on. A decision given cannot be considered a fair, just and reasonable one until and unless the reasons related to it are been provided and if not then it will violate "Articles 14 - Right to Equality" and "Article 21 - Right to Life and Personal Liberty" of the Indian Constitution. "M.J. Sivani v. State of Karnataka" is a case where the court gave its judgement that that when statute prescribe that reasons must be provided, it is a condition precedent to validate an order and also it must be communicated to the party which is being affected.

"It has 3 grounds on which it depends:

1. It helps or fulfill the party against whom order is been passed. The ability to decline to reveal reasons on the side of the request is of an extraordinary nature and it should be practiced reasonably, sparingly and just when completely legitimized by the exigencies of an uncommon situation.
2. The duty to record reasons fills in as obstructions against discretionary action by the judicial power vested in the executive authority.
3. The parties abused gets the opportunity to show before the appellate court the reasons which persuaded the ability to excuse his case weren't right."

NEED FOR REASONED DECISIONS

It presents decency in the regulatory forces and also help to avoid or if nothing else limits arbitrariness. It helps to provide the reasons for the right, which is the basic necessity for the judicial system to be sound and just. It is also deemed to be outstanding amongst other act of good administration.

It entitles the parties with the explanation behind the decision along with the decision itself which is the most important feature of this. It offers satisfaction to the individual against whom the decision has been given and also empowers the individual against whom the decision has been given to look at and utilize his privilege to appeal effectively.

"The Supreme Court observed in Siemens Engg. Vs. Union of India, The rule requiring reasons to be given in support of an order is like the principle of 'Audi alteram partem', a basis principle of natural justice, which must inform every quasi-judicial process and this rule must be observed in its proper spirit and mere pretence of compliance with it would not satisfy the requirement of law."

REASONS MAY BE MANDATED BY THE CONSTITUTION

It has been reiterated by the courts that reasons were necessary as they were the mandate of the constitution in light of the different facts of the case. In certain cases, it is seen, if there is absence of any legislative requirement, providing a reason is a requirement by the Constitution.

The case of "Anumathi Sadhukhan v. A.K. Chatterjee", raises the validity of "Clauses 9 and 13 of West Bengal Rice Mills Control Order, 1949" because the said clause without providing any reasons authorized the authority to issue or renew a license or even cancel or suspend the license. It was challenged on the ground that such an order does not provide for speaking order and also imposed an unreasonable restriction on the fundamental rights of the people. So herein the "Calcutta High court" decided that the said validity of the law was held to be unconstitutional under "Article 19(I)(g) of the Indian Constitution" as it imposed reasonable restriction on the people and also violated the fundamental rights.

REASONS MAY BE MANDATED BY LAW

Reasons that will be required by the law, are considered to be mandatory. There is a plethora of laws which mandate them for the administrative action.

For example- If we take into consideration "Section 31 of the Arbitration and Conciliation Act, 1996", it is necessary for the arbitrator to provide reasons for the awards given. The law states, such reasons which are mandatory to be given and if not provided will be against the law and it will vitiate the action of the administration.

REASONS MAY BE MANDATED BY THE PRINCIPLES OF NATURAL JUSTICE

If some serious bias has been cause, reasons must be mandated by "The Principles of Natural Justice". Most of the time, such situation comes forward when a person suffers a serious bias but the law is silent on the same. Hence, it is required that judicial, administrative as well as quasi-judicial decisions by the court are given along with the reasons for the higher good of the person and maintaining the law and order even if there is not requirement of the same. The same can be observed in the case of "Dev Dutta v Union of India" where a person was not given promotion despite of the fact that he had good entry in the records only due to the reason the other persons had much better entry than him.

However, on investigation it came to light that the entries of good record are not required to be communicated to the person and only the bad ones have to be put in light. The SC gave its decision that the person should not suffer prejudice due to the non-communication and hence the good entry must also be communicated to the person. Also, transparency along with good governance is the third principle of the PNJ besides the other two.

<u>REASONS MAY BE MANDATED BY THE NATURE OF FUNCTIONS</u>

Nature of Functions is another reason where reasoned decisions may be mandated which an administrative authority is exercising. It means if any authority is exercising some "quasi-judicial" functions or if it is evident that appeal or revision is required against the discretions of the authority, reasoned decisions must be provided. In the decision given by apex court in "Mahabir Prasad v. State of U.P"., it was emphasized on the same notion that if any authority is giving any decision regards to quasi-judicial order, reasons must be provided even if it is not been required by the statute.

<u>CONCLUSION</u>

The Principle of Natural Justice has been emphasized in order to maintain rights of the public against the arbitrary power of the authorities. The main goal is to provide justice which is fair, reasonable and just. So, accordingly if the reasons are not being provided properly it will lead to an arbitrary action and if an action is arbitrary it automatically violates "Article 14 of the constitution" which is the basis of "Principles of Natural Justice". So giving of reasons have been made mandatory as shown by various case laws and all disciplinary matters reasons are absolutely mandatory. Hence, it is very important to provide rights to the people.

<u>Author's Biography</u>

A Passionate Law Student with excellent oral and written communication skills and an aim to make a difference through the power of words.

CHAPTER TWENTY-SEVEN

EXTRADITION: THE NATURE OF STATE'S OBLIGATION

Author: Ananaya Chauhan, IV year of B.A.,LL.B from Delhi Metropolitan Education, Noida Affiliated To Guru Gobind Singh Indraprastha University, Delhi.

INTRODUCTION

Extradition is a formal, diplomatic process under international law in which one state demands that another return custody of a fugitive criminal for offenses punishable by the requesting State's laws and committed beyond the jurisdiction of the country where the fugitive has found sanctuary. Because of advancements in air-traffic technology, it is now conceivable for a person to flee to another state after committing a crime in his own. Extradition is the legal process by which a suspect or convicted criminal is handed over to another country or jurisdiction. Extradition is governed by treaties that exist between nations. When Asylum Begins, Extradition Ends. International extradition is a good-faith commitment made by states to promote and carry out justice.

Belgium established the first legal statute providing for extradition in 1833, along with the first legislation on the right to refuge. Extradition Acts define the link between the Act and the treaty by specifying extraditable offenses, as well as processes and protections. Some countries authorize extradition petitions if they have exchanged reciprocity declarations with the seeking countries. Despite the fact that there has been a pattern of resisting extradition petitions in the absence of a binding international agreement between the states, fugitives are frequently surrendered on the basis of local law or as an act of good faith by the State Parties. However, because of the ambiguity, non-parties to extradition treaties may provide a safe refuge for fugitives.

The presence of a binding extradition agreement and the municipal laws of the nation from which extradition is requested are two elements that influence the extradition procedure. Extradition involves two states, for example, the territorial state - the state where an accused or convicted person is located and to whom the request is submitted. Another state has made a request, such as the state where the crime was committed which is the requesting state. The request is submitted through the diplomatic channel, as is customary.

EXTRADITION PURPOSE

A criminal is extradited to the requesting state for the following reasons:

- Extradition is based on the broad principle that it is in the interests of civilized communities for criminals to be brought to justice, and as such it is recognized as a part of the comity of nations that one state should ordinarily provide assistance to another state in bringing offenders to justice.
- Extradition has a deterrence impact because it warns criminals that they will not be able to avoid punishment by fleeing to another country.
- Criminals are handed over in order to protect the territorial state's interests.

- Extradition is carried out because it is a step toward achieving international cooperation in the resolution of worldwide social issues.
- Extradition is founded on the principle of reciprocity.
- Because evidence is more easily available in that State only, the State on whose territory the crime was committed is in a stronger position to prosecute the criminal.

EXTRADITION OF A POLITICAL CRIMINAL IS NOT POSSIBLE

During the French Revolution, the habit of not extraditing political convicts began. Other countries followed suit after that. A political crime has yet to be defined by any commission or body. International law does not define this term either. However, in our own terms, we may explain that if a person commits a crime for political reasons, such action is a political crime.

A prisoner was accused with the murder of Luigi Rossi in the "Re Castioni case (1891)". The killer made his way to England from Switzerland. The British government turned down Switzerland's request for extradition. According to the court, the accused murdered in order to incite political unrest, and so committed a political crime. Because he was a political criminal, England was under no obligation to extradite him.

However, on the contrary, a fugitive who detonated a bomb in a public place in Paris, "Re Meunier Case, 1894", fled to England. Paris wanted him returned, but England refused to extradite him. The court decided that his motives were not solely political, and that he had not committed a political crime as a result.

CLAUSE OF D'ATTENTAT

The d'attentat, or Belge clause, provides that the assassination of leaders of countries or nations is not considered a political crime, and that they can be extradited for it.

RULE OF SPECIALITY

International law recognizes the notion of specialty. It stipulates that a person who is extradited to a nation to face criminal charges can only be prosecuted for those charges and not for any additional pre-extradition offenses.

This concept was reaffirmed in the decision of "United States vs. Rauscher (1886)", which said that he can only be tried for crimes that are criminalized by the treaty and/or the crimes for which extradition is requested.

DOUBLE CRIMINALITY

According to the concept of double criminality, a criminal can only be extradited to another country if the crime he committed is punishable under both countries' laws. For example, if a murderer flees Bangladesh and hides in India, he can be extradited because both nations' laws make murder illegal.

THE STATE'S LEGAL POSITION IN INTERNATIONAL LAW

It is important to highlight that the state has no obligation to extradite a person. However, there might be an agreement between the two countries that any criminals who flee to their nation will be extradited and vice versa. They can also extradite a person without the need for a treaty. States should remember that during extradition, they should not break their own domestic rules, such as national laws and international agreements.

Countries, on the other hand, are not obligated to return fugitives if legitimate extradition procedures were not followed. Mr Vinayak Donador Savarkar was detained by the French navy in the case of "Sarvarkar (1911)".

He was later extradited to England; however, he was obtained via erroneous extradition processes in the United Kingdom. The French demanded his return due to a procedural violation.

The court ruled that under international law, there is no clause stating that if extradition processes are not followed, the government must return him.

Citizens of their own country cannot be extradited by the state. So, if an English person comes to India and commits a crime before fleeing to England, it will be extremely difficult to bring the person back. They generally guarantee that the perpetrator will be punished in accordance with their own laws.

In "Regina vs Wilson (1878)", a treaty between the two nations can be reached, in which the governments agree not to extradite persons and the fugitive would be prosecuted by their own laws.

INDIA

Typically, each nation has its own rules governing the extradition procedure. The Extradition Act of 1962 oversees the extradition procedure in India. Act 66, enacted in 1993, and made changes to it.

Treaties for extradition are discussed under Section 2(d) of the Act, which authorizes foreign countries to negotiate such agreements with India. These treaties are generally bilateral in nature, meaning they only apply to two nations.

Five principles are embodied in these treaties:

- Extradition of a fugitive will take place for crimes listed in the treaty.
- The offense must be made illegal under both nations' laws, not just one.
- A prima facie case must be established.
- The government should only prosecute the convict for the crime for which he was extradited.
- He must be put on trial in a fair manner.

Extradition requests on behalf of India are usually submitted by the Ministry of External Affairs and not by the general public.

Countries that have signed an extradition pact with India can request extradition from India. A non-treaty nation must follow the procedures described in Section 3(4) of the Extradition Act of 1962.

The following are the barriers or impediments to extradition, according to the Ministry of External Affairs' page:

- Unless a treaty exists, India is not obligated to extradite someone.
- Unless the offence is a criminal under the treaty, India is not obligated to extradite someone.
- For solely political and military offenses, extradition may be prohibited.
- Both India and the nation requesting extradition must consider the offense to be a criminal.
- When the method outlined in "Section 3(4) of the Extradition Act of 1962" is not followed, extradition may be rejected.

<u>CONCLUSION</u>

"Extradition is therefore the handover of persons whom it is wanted to deal with from one state to another for crimes of which they have been charged or convicted and are justifiable in the courts of the other state." The Extradition Act of 1962 governs extradition in India and lays out the process. Extradition requires that countries engage into an agreement, known as a treaty that governs the extradition procedure. Sections 41, 166A, 166B, and 188 of the Code of Criminal Procedure outline several extradition processes. Extradition is thus controlled by a number of legislation and treaties. In the nutshell, we can conclude that the law of extradition is important for maintaining peace and order in the society and it is also beneficial for punishing the offenders who were trying to escape from their punishment.

<u>Author's Biography</u>

A Passionate Law Student with excellent oral and written communication skills and an aim to make a difference through the power of words.

CHAPTER TWENTY-EIGHT

JUDICIAL ACTIVISM

<u>Author</u>: Varun Maheshwari, B.B.A.,LL.B from Global Jindal Law School.

The term "Judicial Activism" was coined by Arthur Schlesinger Jr. in 1947 when he used it in Fortune Magazine in his article "The Supreme Court: 1947".There are a lot of interpretations for Judicial Activism. Wharton's Concise Law Dictionary defines 'Judicial Activism' as a situation when judges allow their personal views about policies to interfere with their decisions.

However, the term has evolved with time and has shaped into basically the Supreme Court overstepping its jurisdiction and legislating into matters which either belongs to the legislative or the executive. Even though people still have utmost faith in the judiciary, I am going to argue that Judicial Activism is rising. S.P. Sathe argues that Judicial Activism is often seen as a necessary evil. However it is still evil and one cannot correct a wrong by committing another wrong. It just appears like a justification as they acknowledge the fact that Judicial Activism is on the rise and it is not a good thing. It may seem like a solution for many problems in the short-run however every coin has two sides and Judicial Activism can also take shape into domination by the judiciary. Demosprudence concerns itself with enhancing the democratic work of the judiciary.

We tend to argue that all the three pillars of the Indian democracy have a system of checks and balances however the judiciary has an upper hand in real life and has been exercising that in the recent times. The very Constitution of India has given enough scope for judicial activism to take place in India. The very articles like Article 142 which allows the Supreme Court to pass decree or order to do complete justice. There is no checks and balances for this article. This article's use can be seen in M Siddiq(D) Thr Lrs v. Mahant Suresh Das & Ors. Another article which puts the Supreme Court on a higher pedestal than the others is article 147 which makes it the ultimate authority to interpret any substantial question of law and the constitution. Once an interpretation has been drawn only the SC can change that. Upendra Baxi hits the nail on its head when he says that the power to interpret laws combined with the power to manipulate the interpretation process is in a sense the power to make laws themselves. We can see how the judiciary has often misused this or overused this. In the case of article 124A, the NJAC was turned down by the judiciary which was seen as a very transparent and democratic methodology over the existing controversial collegium system for the appointment of the judges. The participation of the Judiciary at the state or the central level in India is very high as compared to different countries throughout the world. Upendra Baxi rightly points out how the Indian Supreme Court has unparalleled powers in the matters of Judicial Review which often take the shape of judicial activism.

In the early stages, the Judiciary was quite "conventional" and was of the ideology to stick to a narrower scope of the laws and the constitution. There were several tussles between the government and the Judiciary in the emergency era. It is often referred to as the first phase of Judicial Activism in India. The case which started the rivalry between them was the Indira Gandhi v. Raj Narain which became a turning point in the history of the judicial journey. The emergency was one of the darkest periods of the Judiciary. The case of ADM Jabalpur v Shivakant(1976) or famously known as the Habeas Corpus case is often the first example which comes into mind when one talks about the Judiciary surrendered to the whims of the government.

The Court allowed the suspension of all the fundamental rights in the case of an emergency. This was seen as a black stain on the image of the judiciary as the judiciary validated all the tyrannical acts of the government. Only Justice Khanna gave a strong-worded dissenting opinion. The amendment of article 71 made the election of Indira Gandhi legitimate due to the retrospective nature of the amendment. To regain the image the court had three options: annul the constitutional amendment and convict Indira Gandhi in Indira Gandhi v Raj Narain; Uphold the Constitutional amendment and also let Indira Gandhi go free from the case or they could do both annul the constitutional amendment a well as convict Indira Gandhi. However, if the Court would have chosen the first option it would have been a direct implication of war between the court and the government which would have harmed the court adversely as the government was really strong and didn't have a strong opposition either. If the court had chosen the third option the public would have stopped trusting the court as the court of justice and would have made the Supreme Court look blind to the whimsical behaviour of the government at hand. Hence the court chose to take a diplomatic view and went with the third option. The suppression of Justice Khanna (dissenting opinion in ADM Jabalpur Case) and appointment of justice Beg as the Chief Justice of India as an example for the Judges to not express dissent. Post the emergency as soon as Moraji Desai government rose to power the Supreme Court started converting itself into an activist court. S.P. Sathe raised a very well-articulated point that the SC realised that the judgements in the emergency era weren't popular and to gain the support of the masses and regain the credibility it once had focussed more on the enforcement of rights. In the process of doing so the court out-rightly took the path of Judicial Activism. The proportion of cases decided in favour of free speech went up with each passing decade for the first four decades of the court's existence . Sudhir Krishnaswamy proves the change for populism by alleging that the Supreme Court chose to enforce rights in 1990 which it wouldn't have in 1980.

Upendra Baxi brilliantly sums it up by saying "the Supreme Court of India as an apex adjudicative bureaucracy, a final arbiter of the 'doings' of other courts in the hierarchy, has now fully emerged as an institutional political actor". In the Keshvanada Bharti Case (1973) the SC interpreted the Legislature's amendment powers in a very restricting way confining those powers and also formulating a theory itself as the "Basic Structure Doctrine".

The amending powers of the parliament under article 368 of the Constitution of India were challenged. The amending powers of the Parliament were upheld by the court in Sri Sankari Prasad Singh Deo v. Union of India and Sajjan Singh v. the State of Rajasthan. In Keshvananda Bharti the Supreme Court held that the parliament could not amend the Basic Structure of the Constitution. This was known as the "Basic Structure Doctrine". This was well within the interpretation rights entitled to the Supreme Court given by the Constitution of India however this methodology of interpretation raises eyebrows as this not only rules the amendment at hand to be null and void which is well within the judicial review's purview but also legislates the restrictions on the amending powers of the Parliament. Even though the Courts are responsible for reviewing and invalidating executive actions and laws passed by the legislative, in this scenario the court not only did so but came up with a new doctrine which was equivalent to a new legislation in practice.

Sathe also interprets Judicial Activism as the liberal interpretation of the provisions of the constitution such as article 21 which has been recently interpreted in a wider context to include several other intrinsic rights. The Puttaswamy Judgement (2017) in which the SC ruled that Article 21 included Right to Privacy where no such terms were used in the original Constitution or even in the discussions of the constituent assembly. One may argue that changes are necessary and rights should evolve with time but they should evolve through a legislative process through the Legislature and not by the judiciary. In the Unni Krishnan vs State of Andhra Pradesh, the Supreme Court of India held that article 21 covered 16 rights in itself. This may come under the purview of interpretational rights of the Supreme Court of India but one must understand that rights set up a positive action against the government. To put 16 fundamental rights through a judicial case seems inappropriate and disturbs the very balance of the separation of the powers given through the constitution. This also falls bad on the concept of democracy as the rights are not expanded by the people who have been chosen by the people but by the Judges. The people now aware of the liberal and active judiciary "seek extraordinary remedies" transcending the inscribed difference between legislation and adjudication.

The very concept of PIL (1976) is the pinnacle of Judicial Activism. PIL was introduced by Justice B.N. Bhagwati and Justice Iyer. It was a relaxation on the concept of Locus Standi. Even though PIL has served the purpose of improving the judiciary's approachability for people in practical life yet the way it came into existence turns a few heads. The Judges can also take a matter suo motu or through letters addressed to them. Several factors connect Judicial Activism and Public Interest Litigations like how one interprets the role of Judges, separation of powers and courts in a democracy especially the Indian democracy. However, the validity of the facts is also very important. Varun Gauri points out that most social and economic matters do not have matters of contention of genuine rights but of positive actions which entail significant expenditures which in-turn affects other branches of the government. It would have been the role of the legislature to introduce that but the judiciary. It is a classic example of Judicial Activism as they overstepped their jurisdiction to legislate. Justice Iyer says "Activism is essential for participative public justice" which shows how the judge that proposed it knew it himself yet chose to stick with the 'necessary evil'. It is believed that the social and economic matters are the prerogatives of the legislative or the executive and giving positive guidelines are just inappropriate judicial activism.

Varun Gauri argues that "policy, environmental and social must emerge from a socio-political process and must be considered in a legitimate forum, not a judicial one". A.K Thiruvengadam documents the criticism of the judiciary's invasion in the legislation on the topic of Public Interest Litigations.

These include the comments of Justice Hidayutullah, Justice Srikrishna and Justice Kaju who stated that the Public Interest Litigation "has developed into an uncontrollable Frankenstein". Roy even goes to the length to say that we live in a "judicial dictatorship" and we don't even know that yet. It is important for us to look beyond the empirical profits of a concept like the PIL and understand the legitimacy of the process behind it and their consequences.

<u>Author's Biography</u>

I am a student of O.P. Jindal Global Law School pursuing law currently in my second year. I have a key inclination towards Judiciary and Civil Law particularly. Arbitration is another field I am currently exploring. My hometown is Bhopal, Madhya Pradesh. I have completed my schooling majorly in Indore and Bhopal. Due to the Covid-19 pandemic, I am yet to visit the college campus through an online manner however I am hopeful that it isn't far now.

EVOLUTION OF COPYRIGHT: AN UNFORTUNATE DAWN?

Author: K. Sri Hamsa, IV year of B.A.,LL.B.(Hons.) from DSNLU, Visakhapatnam

Co-author: Sri Vaishnavi.M.N, IV year of B.A.,LL.B.(Hons.) from DSNLU, Visakhapatnam

Any creative invention of mind or innovative inventions of mind can be known as the Intellectual Property for starters. It can be new music, design, or a specific product which is a new invention and is a direct outcome of mind. Now, it is a general tendency of a human being to copy or take whatever he/she is unable to procure, let it be a resource or a design or maybe we could also go to an extent where a human being couldn't be able to procure an object or an idea which was invented too.

That is a juncture of thought when he/she tries to obtain it by force. Law, to a greater extent, protects the civilisation from chaos. As UNESCO states "War begins in the minds of men"[i]and also it had given various approaches to create peace and harmony in the minds of men and women which can be observed in its preamble itself.[ii]Today, it is the same mind that the law itself is trying to protect, the same mind, but one with innovation.

As the 26th United States President, Theodore Roosevelt has stated that "No man is above the law, No man is below it; nor do we ask any man's permission when we ask him to obey it,"[iii]Law is a social instrument which is a powerful one to win over chaos. It is an authority to which everyone is bound to be liable to. Having said the greatest prominence, the latest laws have been to a greater extent developed in such a manner that it has also dealt with Intellectual Property.

After a higher deliberation, we could determine that Intellectual Property, especially Copyright, is an outcome of Innovation and Creativity consisting of concrete ideas which needs to be protected in order to avoid the wars in the minds of men of today's timeline. Intellectual Property is the foundation of almost every new element which seems to be providing an ease of lifestyle for all the individuals, ranging from the software in our phones to the designs of various products we use.

However, ever since the earliest timelines, this optimistic view towards Intellectual Property was never a wholesome aspect. The third United States President, Thomas Jefferson has opined specifically on Intellectual Property that "He who receives an idea from me, receives instruction himself without lessening mine; as he who lights his taper at mine, receives light without darkening me."[iv]

Speaking in a broader and modern sense today, Thomas Jefferson actually sounded inclined towards open-source licensing which we follow today in various types of information databases. We could also approach it in a very orthodox manner by limiting his thought to the concept of "idea" itself. Either way, this is some way we could sense the evolution in Intellectual Property.

The Million Dollar Question following every innovation is that "Is it in the Public Interest?" Our analysis in the following context deals with the advantages/disadvantages of the evolution of Intellectual Property Rights vastly in relation to the Indian Laws.

<u>Protection of Public Interest Through Fair Use Doctrine</u>

When the issue of Public Interest comes to the debate at a very simple stage, we can state that it can be left to be determined with the interpretation of the law with the compatible facts and circumstances of the case. Now, in a very best-case approach, we could start by analysing the interpretation of the Hon'ble Supreme Court of India when it comes to the protection of Intellectual Property over Public Interest.

During the nascent stages of awareness towards various Intellectual Property Laws and also during the golden period of technological evolution, there has been a rising importance for databases too. And one such technologically innovative approach of a company has resulted in various copyright infringement suits from the company against the respondents who have copied and attempted to distribute its work. In the case of Eastern Book Company v. D.B. Modak, it has been held by the Hon'ble Supreme

Court of India in the year of 2007 that the concept of "Minimal Level of Creativity" is still enough for the Appellants to obtain copyright under the Copyright Act.[v]

The Supreme Court has clearly been able to distinguish the concept of "Minimum Originality" with the doctrine of "Sweat of the Brow." Also, a factor to consider in this regard is that this Landmark Case still might not have addressed the factor of Public Access to the subsisted Copyright. Additionally, it is definitely not the right approach to follow the Fairness Theory and Welfare Theory in an independent manner owing to the primary reason that they both might still be co-dependent in a mixed socialist economy such as India.

However, from another perspective or when we look at it from another angle of this, there were many instances when there is an actual conflict between the Public Access and the Intellectual Property Rights such as the copyrights for a particular text, lyrics etc. which has an extent of innovation in it. Our aim through this blog is to analyse the Intellectual Property law from various dimensions and primarily relate it to the concept of fair use doctrine which has been enshrined in Section 52 of the Indian Copyright Act, 1957.[vi]

In relation to Section 52 of the Act,it is basically essential for us to understand the instances where the issue of copyright infringement arises and at which point exactly does it conflict with Section 52. The first Landmark Case Law which had addressed this issue was in the Hon'ble Delhi High Court in India TV Independent News Service Pvt. Ltd v. Yashraj Films Pvt. Ltd. which took place on 21st August, 2012.[vii]

The Delhi High Court, then, upon the reference of various other Landmark Case Laws in foreign jurisdictions and after the consideration of the Facts and Circumstances of the Case has obtained a four-factor test to be applied to all the cases in the conflict of copyright infringement wherein these 4 factors can also, in another words, be treated as exemptions to the copyright infringement.[viii]

Therefore, if the usage of any copyrighted product falls under the ambit of these four factors, then it cannot be determined that the copyright has been infringed. The four factors are as follows-

1. The purpose and the character of the use, including whether such use is of a commercial nature or is for non-profit educational purposes;
2. The nature of the copyrighted work;

3. The amount and substantiality of the portion used in relation to the copyrighted work as a whole; and

4. The effect of the use upon the potential market or value of the copyrighted work.[ix]

And, as we will see later, fair use is determined on the same four factors in India as it is in the United States. Lastly, the Hon'ble Delhi High Court had discussed in-depth about the Fair Use Doctrine and had dismissed the applications for the interim injunction prayed for with the reasoning that there is an increasing number of inconsequential copyright violations across the country and it is our opinion today that it is a very fortunate aspect that the Delhi High Court has viewed the society's best interest in the present judgement.[x]

The Delhi High Court has termed three reasons for the rise in the trivial copyright violations which are-

1. Smaller amount of "Modicum of Creativity" will suffice for a cognizance/grant of copyright.

2. Presence of Unregistered Copyright. For example, u/s. 15 of the Copyright Act, Designs are deemed to be protected under the Copyright Act up to 50 times of its usage. The owner of that specific design needs to get the design registered for the copyright before exercising exploitation on the design for the 51st time.

3. Statutory Rights are broader for the copyright holders.

The Delhi High Court has stated that the Fair Use Doctrine is very much important in today's scenario keeping in mind these trivial copyright violations. The High Court has pointed out that in the absence of a doctrine, even the simplest of the aspects might still be a copyright violation. Therefore, it is from the context of the judgement from the abovementioned Landmark Case Law, we learn that society's best interests often weigh over the copyright holder who wishes to create a monopoly over his/her inventions.

<u>Genesis of Fair Use Doctrine</u>

The main issue or in another term, the root cause or solution for these Landmark Case Laws regarding the Copyright, which is an actual kind of an Intellectual Property Right can be found in the doctrine of Fair Use. The Doctrine of Fair Use can be historically observed in the United States wherein there were many Landmark Case Laws discussing this aspect in the early 1960s. The Legal Position before the advent of the doctrine of Fair Use was really settled in nature.

Then, the Courts used to interpret which usage constituted Fair Use and which didn't in the copyright cases. However, with technological advancement, even the most technologically sophisticated infrastructure still has a narrower loophole left behind and also today, we live in a data-sensitive world where, unfortunately, even famous people have their social media accounts hacked.

Therefore, envisaging this advancement as a necessity for stronger measures and to avoid repercussions of various decisions by the Courts in the future, the Royal Council (Congress) in the United States had codified the doctrine of Fair Use and had developed four factors which can also be considered as a "Test" in the simple language to identify if a work has been a fair use and whether it amounts to a copyright infringement or not.[xi]

When we observe the author's viewpoint about the doctrine of Fair Use in the above-cited article, he has believed that the four factors which determined the nature of fair use in copyright cases are translucent and were not clear at context initially. However, when we see into his views further on, we could observe that the Supreme Court of the United States in the Landmark Case of Campbell v. Acuff-RoseMusic Inc had declared and adjudicated that the result of the issue regarding the aspect of Fair Use in any given case will be dependent on the four factors which have been given by the Royal Council (Congress).[xii]

This Case Law has also been observed by the Delhi High Court in Super Cassettes Industries Ltd. v. Mr. Chintamani Rao &Ors. This Case Law deals with the infringement of copyright of audio and music lyrics wherein the Delhi High Court has time and again emphasised the importance of the four-factor test in order to determine the fair use of a copyright. Still, after an extravagant discussion between us, one question still persists which is "Whether Fair Use Doctrine provides for an unlimited infringement of copyright when it is in conflict with the Public Interest?" for which we would be analysing this aspect in terms of the core Public Interest angle in the further contexts of this blog.[xiii]

Copyright v. Public Interest

Copyright infringement which meets the criteria within the ambit of Section 52 of the Act can be considered as Fair use, for example, copyrighted works can be used for educational purposes but if there is any commercial use under this pretext then the defendants cannot take under the defence of Section 52. "In Super Cassettes Industries Ltd. v. Chintamani Rao[xiv]and Super Cassettes Industries Ltd. v. Hamar Television Network Pvt. Ltd.[xv], regarding the defence of fair dealing, the Court applied the "commercial exploitation test"(which is the first factor) and observed that if a publisher commercially exploits the original work and infringes on the copyright in the process, the defence of fair dealing would not be available to such a publisher, even if the book published by him is used, or intended to be used, for research or private study."

To understand the above-mentioned issue and the question of whether public interest can outweigh the rights of the owner, we will analyse the recent case of Elsevier ltd. v. Alexandra Elbakyan,[xvi]where three publishing companies filed a suit against two websites namely Sci Hub owned by Alexandra Elbakyan (herein Defendant No.1), a computer programmer from Kazakhstan and Libgen or Library Genesis (herein Defendant No.2). Most of the publications of the plaintiff companies need a subscription, ensuring that copyright owners/authors receive some credit for the same. Defendant No.1 claims that the objective behind the creation of Sci Hub is to provide a unlimited public access to tens of millions of research papers and it has over 85 million publications while defendant 2 claims that they help a user to find a particular article or book being a links aggregator and it has accessibility to over 85 million journal articles and 2.8 million textbooks.

The plaintiffs contended that they have exclusive rights by means of agreements with the authors/owners of the works guaranteed under "Article 14(a)(i), (ii) and (iii) of the Copyright Act, 1957[xvii]i.e., to reproduce, to issue copies and to perform the work in public or communicate it respectively." They also contended that the defendants' acts led to copyright infringement under Sections 51 (a), 51(b)(i), (ii) and (iii)of the Copyright Act[xviii]as they did not have any authority or licence to publish such work and that they affected the owners of the copyright and the publishers violating their exclusive rights with respect to the copyrighted work. They have also invoked Section 65A[xix]and 65B of the Copyright Act[xx]for circumventing the protection of copyright provided under the Act through a technological measure and remove and distribute the information without any authority as such.

The plaintiffs highly relied on the case of UTV Software Communication Ltd. v. 1337 X. to &Ors.[xxi]where the Delhi High Court has declined the idea of "internet exceptionalism" stating that the internet should also be regulated and cannot be excluded from reasonable restrictions. The court has discussed "whether blocking a website dedicated to piracy is against free and open internet" and it was held that the freedom of using and publishing on the internet must be regulated by drawing necessary lines to confine access to such infringing websites. It was added that the freedom and the rights of all the stakeholders must be balanced.

The Court has also explained the idea of rogue websites which are mainly built by sharing content which has been infringed, this includes music and film piracy. It was elaborated that a rouge website can be identified by determining some factors including whether the website primarily aims at copyright infringement, responds appropriately to a takedown notice for copyright infringing content, receives a significant amount of traffic, and posts guidelines on the website to circumvent measures that disable access to the website based on related copyright infringement, and so on

The Court then defined the criteria for identifying what constitutes a rogue website. Two globally recognized tests for determining a 'rogue website' are compared and contrasted. In developing a criterion appropriate for the Indian setting, the Court considered two competing viewpoints previously adopted by Indian courts in two different landmark cases. In Eros International Media Ltd. &Anr. v. Bharat Sanchar Nigam Ltd. &Ors.,[xxii]the Bombay High Court stated that blocking injunctions against complete websites may only be issued if the Plaintiff provided proof that the entire website comprised of only unlawful or illicit content. In cases where blocking orders were requested, the Bombay High Court established a three-pronged verification test that courts had to follow. In contrast, the Delhi High Court's division bench in Department of Electronics and Information Technology v. Star India Pvt. Ltd.,[xxiii](which was ultimately relied on in the Sci Hub Case) took a more practical, qualitative approach in determining a rogue website as one that is largely infringing. The Court determined that the quantitative approach used to adopt a three-step verification criterion is too cumbersome to copyright owners, particularly in circumstances when websites change URLs after being prohibited. In such a circumstance, finding each violating and infringing URL would be a massive and nearly impossible undertaking for the copyright owner. As a result, the Court determined that the Defendant Websites were rogue. The Court decided that a blocking injunction against the entire website is lawful, but that courts must follow proportionality in doing so. The onus is on the right holders to show that any website sought to be blocked is a 'rogue website' mainly engaged in assisting widespread copyright infringement to the satisfaction of the Court.

The defendants in the Sci Hub Case contended that their acts fall under the exclusive domain of Section 52 of the Indian Copyright Act[xxiv]and it comes under fair dealing as the intention behind the website is to create access to researchers stating that there should be free access to knowledge. Researchers and other people who support the free access of the publications are citing the case of the Chancellor, Masters & Scholars of the University of Oxford &Ors. v. Rameshwari Photocopy Services &Ors,[xxv]also known as the "DU Photocopying case". In this case, a suit was filed against a photocopy shop in the premises of Delhi University in the context that they are involved in photocopying of the copyrighted work without any authority or license. The suit was rejected by the Delhi High Court stating that the act falls within the ambit Section 52(1)(i) of the Copyright Act as the copies were made for educational purposes.

While the supporters of Sci hub website (citing DU Photocopy case) contend that this also comes within the ambit of Section 52, the opposers contend that exception cannot be claimed as Sci Hub provides copyrighted material for anyone who wants to access and that it might not necessarily be used for educational purposes. However, in Super Cassettes Industries Ltd. v. Hamar Television Network Pvt. Ltd[xxvi]the court held that "in certain circumstances, the public interest may be so compelling that courts will not hesitate in injuncting use of even "leaked information" or the right to use the "very words" in which the aggrieved person has copyright, as public interest may require the use of the "very words" to convey the message to the general public. While courts may refuse to issue injunctions based on the concept of freedom of speech, this does not necessarily protect the infringer in a lawsuit brought on behalf of the person who is the rightful owner of the copyright for damages and an account of profits." Interestingly, this concept is a double-edged knife. Even if the courts rely on this precedent and do not grant an injunction order against Sci hub and Libgen, this nonetheless might not be enough to protect from being held liable for the damages caused due the said copyright infringement.

Still there is no judgment delivered as such in the case of Sci Hub. Can Sci-hub not be held liable for copyright infringement with the mere defence under Section 52 of the Copyright Act? Does the Sci Hub website come under the ambit of Fair dealing? Would an increase in the traffic to the Sci-hub website doesn't commercially benefit the owner? Would this pass the commercial exploitation test or would it still be an exception? The whole objective behind copyright law is to protect the rights of the author/owner and will this objective not be hindered by providing such exceptions under Section 52 especially where there are millions of publications without authorization meaning equal number of copyright infringements? Does the Sci hub objective fall within the ambit of Article 27(1) of UDHR[xxvii]i.e., everyone has right to enjoy and share the benefits of scientific advancement making this a human right issue or does the rights of the rightful author prevail as per Article 27(2) of UDHR[xxviii]i.e., everyone has the right to protection of moral and material interests resulting from scientific, artistic or literary work/production as an author/owner of such work?

These are some of the questions that will only be clearly answered after an interpretation is made by the Hon'ble Delhi High Court. The judgment would also, presumably, clarify the rights and duties of the academic publishers, set guidelines for usage of copyrighted work under Section 52 of the Copyright Act, 1957 and the distinction between piracy and online sharing.

<u>Conclusion</u>

The most awaiting Judgment by the Hon'ble Delhi High Court is the silver lining in our view to analyse the evolution of Indian Copyright Act, 1957 and the concept of Copyright in IP Regime. The socio-legal flavour adds on at a juncture of context in this blog wherein from a certain extent, the copyrights of genuine hard-working researchers are at stake and they are unable to derive the fruits of the seeds sown.

Ultimately, it all boils down to the factor of Public Interest v. Copyright and it is a unique jurisprudence which lies and describes about the prevalence of either one of the concepts which also rests down upon the interpretation of the Hon'ble Delhi High Court. Finally, something that can be agreed upon by the society as a whole is the true saying by Teddy Roosevelt that No man is above the law. In modern terms, under Delhi High Court, it might also be probably understood that No Rogue Website is above the law and has to abide by the same wherein the concept of Public Interest Prevails.

On the other hand, the Delhi High Court might also give greater value and importance to the concept of an "Idea" construed as "Taper" in the words of the 3rd President of the United States of America, Thomas

Jefferson, wherein the President gave value to a shared innovation and that such shared innovation has no probability of darkening the civilization in the future prospects.

It is still a wilder ambiguity as to the fact that whether websites like Sci Hub are still a true taper which shares light among the whole research community or is it just another black cat in a dark room, an abstract which is unsolvable?

CHAPTER THIRTY

ROLE OF PRESIDING OFFICER OR SPEAKER OF THE PARLIAMENT AND LEGISLATIVE ASSEMBLY-RESPECT TO ANTIDEFECTION LAW IN INDIA

Author: Anuja Rajam Cherian, Advocate, Trivandrum Bar Association

ABSTRACT

The role of speaker/presiding officer is vital for a smooth functioning of government. The Speaker/Presiding Officer is the guardian of the rights and privileges of the House, its committees and members.The entire Parliamentary Estate is under the authority of the Speaker.[1]The Speaker has certain residuary powers under the Rules of Procedure. All matters which are not specifically provided under the rules and all questions relating to the working of the rules are regulated by him/her.In exercise of this power and under his/her inherent powers, the Speaker issues from time-to-time directions which are generally treated as sacrosanct as the Rules of Procedure.Under the Constitution, the Speaker/Presiding Officer enjoys a special position insofar as certain matters pertaining to the relations between the two Houses of Parliament and Legislative Assemblies are concerned. In the 52nd Constitution amendment, the Speaker/Presiding Officer is vested with the power relating to the disqualification of a member of the Lok Sabha/Raj Sabha on grounds of defection.Paragraph 6 of the Tenth Schedule empowers the Speaker/Presiding Officer to decide upon the questions of disqualification. The Anti-Defection Law is clear that the question of disqualification or otherwise under the Tenth Schedule is to be decided by the Speaker/Presiding Officer. The Courts have only the power of judicial review and any a priori intervention is ruled out.It is an established precedent that the Speaker as the Head of Legislature and being a constitutional authority is not amenable to the jurisdiction of the Courts.However, this applies in respect of the conduct of legislative business where the Speaker is supreme and final authority. Hence, the Speaker/Presiding Officer must be a person with expertise in constitutional laws.

The Tenth Schedule provides presiding officers/ speakers of Parliament/ legislatures with the power to decide cases of defection. Many a times the decisions of the Presiding Officers with regard to disqualifications have been challenged before courts for being biased and partial.TheSupreme Court has upheld the provision granting the Presiding officer the power to takethe decisions on the ground that the Presiding Officers hold a pivotal position in the scheme of parliamentarydemocracy and are guardians of the rights and privileges of the House.

<u>POWERS OF SPEAKER/CHAIRMAN/PRESIDING OFFICER</u>

Paragraph 6 of the tenth schedule of the Constitution provides that questions relating to disqualification of member of the house shall be referred to the Speaker whose decisionon the same will be final. Any question regarding disqualification arising out ofdefection is to be decided by the Presiding Officer of the House. According to paragraph2(1)(a) of the Tenth Schedule of the Constitution, an elected member of the houseshall be disqualified from being a member if they win the election as a candidate of oneparty and then join another.[1] The power for this disqualification is vested in the Speaker,who is usually a nominee of the ruling party.

Interestingly, a discussion is already underway among presiding officers of legislatureson how to secure the legislative Speaker's "dignity" in the matters related to thedefection of lawmakers.[2]Former Lok Sabha secretary TK Vishwanathan said that the anti-defection law has putthe entire onus on the Speaker in the matters related to disqualification of members ofthe Legislative House. Even if the Speaker is impartial, he faces undue pressure andcriticism.There are instances such as these. In a state in India: the single-largest party with twenty-eight (28) seats, was three seats short of the majority markin the sixty (60)-seat assembly, could not able to form a government. The second positionsecured by another party, with twenty-one (21) seats, moved to stake claim along with the regionalparties. One of the members of the initially majority party extended supportto the next major party, helping to form a coalition government. The defector was madea minister of town planning, forest and environment in the new government.At leastthirteen (13) petitions were filed by the majority party who secured the maximum seatsin the Legislative Assembly before the Speaker. But the Speaker did not act on thecomplaints. Two Member of Legislative Assemblies, next approached the ManipurHigh Court. The High Court noted the seriousness of the issue but declined to grant anyrelief on the ground that the issue regarding powers of High Court to interfere with theSpeaker's discretion is pending before Supreme Court.[3]The aggrieved party then moved the Supreme Court in appeal. The Speaker of theLegislative Assembly argued before the Supreme Court that the issue regarding whetherHigh Courts can direct Speakers to decide a disqualification petitions within a particulartime frame was referred to a constitution bench of the Supreme Court in 2015 in thecase of SA Sampath Kumar v. Kale Yadaiah[4]. Hence, he submitted, the decision in theManipur case should be deferred till the constitution bench decides the issue.However, the Supreme Court turned down this argument holding that the issue wasconclusively settled by the top court in a 2007 judgment of Rajendra Singh Rana v.Swami Prasad Maurya[5]in which the court ruled that the High Court can direct Speakersto rule on disqualification petitions if they do not do this within a reasonable time. Theapex court directed the Speaker of the Manipur assembly to rule on the disqualificationpleas pending before him within four weeks. The court also made it clear that if theSpeaker does not take a decision within four weeks, it will be open to any party to applyto the Supreme Court for further relief.

The Speaker of the House enjoys vast powers on disqualificationproceedings, with the Supreme Court consistently holding that it would not interfere insuch proceedings until the Speaker actually makes a decision. One of the first cases inthis regard was a 1992 judgment, when the court asserted that "having regard to theConstitutional Schedule in the Tenth Schedule, judicial review should not cover anystage prior to the making of a decision by the Speakers/Chairmen". The majority heldthat the power to resolve disputes vested in the Speaker or Chairman by the TenthSchedule is a judicial power and Paragraph 6(1) is valid to the extent it seeks to impartfinality to their decision. The majority in Kihito Hollohan case also rejected thecontention that the vesting of adjudicatory functions in the Speakers/Chairmen wouldby itself vitiate the provision on the ground of likelihood of political bias. The dissentingminority, however, held that constitutional scheme contemplates adjudication onquestions of disqualification of elected members by independent authorities outside theHouse, i.e., President/Governor in accordance with the opinion of the ElectionCommission, all of whom are high constitutional functionaries with security of tenureindependent of the will of the House.

Once the factsgathered or placed show that a member of the House has done any such act which comeswithin the purview of para 2(1), (2) or (3) of the Schedule,[6] the disqualification willapply and the Chairman or the Speaker of the House will have to make a decision to thateffect.The law does not specify a time-period for the Presiding Officer to decide on adisqualification plea. There have been several cases where the Courts haveexpressed concern about the unnecessary delay in deciding such petitions. In 2012Speaker Haryana Vidhan Sabha Vs Kuldeep Bishnoi & Ors Court expressed concernsover the delays.[7] In some cases, this delay in decision making has resulted in members,who have defected from their parties, continuing to be members of the House. Therehave also been instances where opposition members have been appointed ministers inthe government while still retaining the membership of their original parties in thelegislature.

PRIVILEDGES OF THE PRESIDING OFFICER/SPEAKER

Speaker as the final arbiter in disqualification proceedings inside theHouse/Legislative Assembly

The speaker cannot initiate a suo-motu petition, it is the final arbiter only in case of apetition moved by a member. In several cases before the Supreme Court, questions areraised regarding the constitutional validity of Paragraph 6(1) which states that thespeaker shall have the final arbiter in proceedings regarding disqualification of amember. In furtherance to its constitutional validity, Supreme Court has asked toprovide clarity upon the nature of the Speaker's power and whether the office of thespeaker will be termed as tribunal. The court in case of Kihoto Hollohan[8]held that since the disqualification proceedingshave two parties against and an authority decides the dispute by use of judicial power,such authority is a tribunal as it does not have all the trappings of a court.Remarking on the growing trend of Speakers acting contrary totheir constitutional duty of being neutral, the Supreme Court held that the Speakercannot either indicate the period for which a person is disqualified, nor bar him fromcontesting elections.In a 31-page judgment, a three-judge Bench led by Justice Rohinton F. Narimanquestioned why a speaker, who is a member of a particular political party and an insiderin the House, should be the "sole and final arbiter" in the disqualification of a politicaldefector. It is time Parliament had a rethink on whether disqualification petitions oughtto be entrusted to a speaker as a quasi-judicial authority when such Speaker continuesto belong to a particular political party either de jure or de facto.

Is there any time limit for decision taken by the Speaker?

The anti-defection law does not specify a timeframe for Speakers to decide on defectionproceedings. When the politics demands, Speakers are either quick to pass judgment ondefection proceedings or delayed acting on them for years on end. However, for the present, the court said the Speakers should decideTenth Schedule disqualifications within a "reasonable period". What is 'reasonable'would depend on the facts of each case.Theconcern party asked the Speaker to disqualify, but the petitions are kept pending.In one of the Southern States, legislators of the main opposition party boycottedthe entire 12-day assembly session. This boycott was in protest against the delay ofover eighteen (18) months in action being taken against legislators of their party who haveallegedly defected to the ruling party. However, in areas wherein the Speaker is expected tofunction as a quasi-judicial authority under the Tenth Schedule, it would definitelyinvite judicial review and the Office of the Speaker cannot claim any special privilege.The Court in Keisham Meghachandra Singh also observed:"In the years that have followed the enactment of the Tenth Schedule in 1985, thisCourt's experience of decisions made by Speakers generally leads us to believe that thefears of the minority judgment in Kihoto Hollohan have actually come home to roost."

Speaker's decisions and Judicial review

The law initially stated that the decision of the Presiding Officer is not subject to judicialreview. This condition was struck down by the Supreme Court in 1992, thereby allowingappeals against the Presiding Officer's decision in the High Court and Supreme Court.Kihoto Hollohan Vs Zachillhu and Others (1992). However, it held that there may notbe any judicial intervention until the Presiding Officer gives his order.Paragraph

7 was the most controversial provision which blatantly attacked as it barredthe jurisdiction of High Courts and Supreme Courts in respect of any matter connectedwith the disqualification of a member of a House under this Schedule. The court in thecase of Kihoto Hollohan held the provision to be unconstitutional as it denies the rightto approach the judiciary as well as of judicial review. Further, under Article 368(2)there requires half of the state legislatures to ratify this provision however no suchratification was received and therefore, the court while applying the doctrine ofseverability, declared Paragraph 7 to be unconstitutional.Two issues were raised that whether the Speaker of a legislature is bound by thedirections of a Court and whether judicial review by courts extends to rules framedunder the Tenth Schedule.It is held by the Hon'ble Apex Court that "the orders passedby a speaker are subject to judicial review and rules under the Tenth Schedule areprocedural in nature. Any violation of those would be a procedural irregularity.Procedural irregularity is immune from judicial scrutiny."A very important issue regarding that when can a court review the Speaker's decision-making process under the Tenth Schedule was answered by the Supreme Court inRajendra Singh Rana and Ors. vs. Swami Prasad Maurya and Ors[9], it was held that ifthe Speaker fails to act on a complaint, or accepts claims of splits or mergers withoutmaking a finding, he fails to act as per the Tenth Schedule. The Court said that ignoringa petition for disqualification is not merely an irregularity but a violation ofconstitutional duties.

The Speaker, in acting as aTribunal under the Tenth Schedule, is bound to decide disqualification petitions withina reasonable period. The Speaker should not stall this matter. Constitutional courtscannot judicially review disqualification proceedings under the Tenth Schedule (anti-defection law) of the Constitution until the Speaker or Chairman makes a final decisionon merits.The Kihoto Hollohan judgment is significant in the case of ousted Rajasthan DeputyChief Minister and other eighteen (18) Member of Legislative Assembly, who were issued noticeunder the anti-defection law after the ruling party sought their disqualification.The Bench explained that the reason for limiting the role of courts in ongoing defectionproceedings is that the office of the Speaker is held in the highest respect and esteemin parliamentary traditions. The evolution of the institution of parliamentary democracyhas as its pivot the institution of the Speaker. He is said to be the very embodiment ofpropriety and impartiality.[10]

Speaker and Issue of Impartiality

The Parliament now has to decide whether the Speaker who himself is a member of aparty should be allowed to decide on membership or not. The office of Speaker has beencriticized time and again for being an agent of partisan politics especially in context ofpower for the disqualification. The Supreme Court in Jagjit Singh versus State ofHaryana[11] highlighted the similar allegations about the confidence on the role ofSpeaker in the matters of impartiality. In the Kihoto Hollohan versus Zachillhu case(1992), one of the judges observed that the suspicion of bias on the Speaker's role couldnot be ruled out as his/her election and tenure depends on the majority will of the House(or specifically of the ruling party).Impartiality, fairness and autonomy in decision-making are the hallmarks of a robustinstitution. It is the freedom from interference and pressures which provide thenecessary atmosphere where one can work with an absolute commitment to the causeof neutrality (as a Constitutional value). At a time when India's rank has fallen in thelatest Democracy Index (2019), it is expected from Parliament to take steps to revampand strengthen the institution of the Speaker. Further, the structural issues regarding themanner of appointment of the Speaker and his tenure in office needs an urgent redressal.On Dec4, 2017 Chairman had disqualified the two rebels from the Rajya Sabha, on aplea filed by the party on Sep 2,2017. The decision was one of the swiftest in the history ofthe Rajya Sabha. The Chairman claimed that disqualification of a member of thelegislature should be decided by the Presiding Officer in about three months to thwartpolitical defections. In the case of the two Member of Parliaments who were disqualifiedfrom Rajya Sabha they were deemed to have 'voluntarily given up their membership'by engaging in anti-party activities which included criticizing the party on public forumson multiple occasions, and attending rallies organized by opposition parties.[12]

Review of Speaker's own decision

In a case, whether a speaker can review his own decision to disqualify amember under the Tenth Schedule, it is held that the Speaker of a House does nothave the power to review his own decisions to disqualify a candidate. Such power is notprovided for under the Schedule, and is not implicit in the provisions either.

Quick Action of Speaker and the 'Destructive of democratic process'

Even as the twin issues of the speaker's inertia and legislators' resignation intertwine,the focus is well and truly on the anti-defection law with most constitutional experts inagreement that the Act needs to be looked at afresh. Says noted constitutional law expertand author Gautam Bhatia: Legislatorsresign and get around the provisions of the Act. This is destructive of democraticprocess. He pointed to the possibility of members switching sides not because ofideological compulsions but because of political blackmail.[13]Advocate Rajneesh Chuni remarked Legislators have become smarter. They do not mergewith another party. They merely resign from their party and circumvent the law.However, the whole burden falls on the common man, the voters who might have votedfor a particular political party, then are dismayed to see their representative resignmidway. They feel cheated. After resignation, the Speaker has to be proactive. Hecannot sit on resignations endlessly. But if the resignations are accepted, elections arethe only way out. There is no Assembly that has not been betrayed in recent years.Under the provisions of the Tenth Schedule to the Constitution, the Presiding Officersof the Houses/Legislative Assemblies have been given the authority to decide questionsof violation of the provisions of the Anti-Defection Law. [14]

While discharging their functions under the Tenth Schedule of the Constitution, thePresiding Officers of the House or Legislative Assembly are treated as Tribunalsexercising specific jurisdiction as conferred by the Schedule. Such exercise of power isdehors the constitutional authority of the Presiding Officers to have exclusivejurisdiction to regulate the proceedings of the House and as such, the Presiding Officersare not immune from their orders being challenged in Courts of Law and in many casesnot only such orders have been set-aside by the judicial authorities but adversecomments have also been made. It has recently appeared in the media that a PresidingOfficer of one of the Legislative Assemblies in our country has been directed by the court to indicate the time within which a pending matter relating to defection will bedisposed of. The petition as a grievance has been made before the Court, it appears fromthe Media, that the concerned Presiding Officer was deliberately delaying the disposalof the matter before him.This category of laws is applicable to both, state assemblies as well as both houses ofthe parliament for the disqualification of the members so as to strengthen the democracy.

The absolute power of the chairman or the speaker has been a bone ofcontentions since its inception of the provision in 1985. This provision has beeninappropriately misused by the power icons to promote corruption and furthermiscarriage of justice by upholding the agenda of the political party they belong to.In most of the cases, the delay in decision of the

Presiding Officer paves way fordefection to be controlled.

Inadequacies of the Law

A human mind is bound to havebiases. The freshly elected legislators elect the speaker of the assembly and hence inalmost all the cases, the speaker is a member of the ruling party. It is the fact that the "tenure of thespeaker depends on the continuous support of the majority present in the house".Though the speaker of the assembly is expected to be free from biases of any sort, justand fair, it cannot be denied that an inherent bias can creep in because of the previouspolitical affiliations. This bias turns into gross injustice when the speaker misuses thispower. This power stems from Paragraph 6 of the schedule that "empowers the speakerto be the decisive arbiter regarding any question pertaining to the disqualification of anymember of the house" under Paragraph 2 of the schedule. Thus, in the garb of being justand fair, the speaker might espouse their political affiliations backhandedly. Andultimately, the decision of the ruling party hidden under the veil of the speaker becomesthe rule. Though the apex court in Jagjit Singh v. State of Haryana[15] stated that thedecision of the speaker is subject to judicial review, it expressly stated that it can bereviewed only one the basis of any procedural lapses in question but not on merits.

Reasonable Time for Final Decision by the Speaker

The Tenth Schedule has not defined about the definite time limits for competition ofdisqualification process of the defecting members. It is found that judiciary is by andlarge helpless at the Pre decisional Stage. There is no time limit. A reasonable timelimit is still a question.Oneof the major causes of delay to take action against the legislators who left the party. Inorder to clarify his role, the Speaker suggests to approach the court, adding that he willact as per the law. The net effect is "The legislature in its wisdom has put no time limiton the Speaker to decide (the matter)".The Supreme court opined that such loopholes and discrepancies that exist in theschedule should be removed. It asked the parliament to reanalyze the 'quasi-judicialauthority' that exists with the speaker of the assembly enshrined in Paragraph 6 of theschedule, considering the fact that he belongs to a particular political party and mayhave his own biases owing to the affiliations.

Speaker does not have the power of disqualifying any member fromContesting election

This event brings upon yet another question relating to the schedule. Neither theprovision of the constitution itself nor any other statues in power bar the disqualifiedmembers from contesting elections. This loophole empowers them to win the seat backvia re-elections crushing the goal of the fair and ideal process. The Speaker in order torefrain the defected members from using this defect for their benefit (in current case-tostand for re-elections), barred them from contesting elections which is not within hispower to decide and is correctly stated ultra vires by the court.[16]

RECOMMENDATIONS

The Speaker of the House to check defections (anti-defection law), specifying a time frame to handle a case, and to take into account the conduct of a member before taking a decision. It is high time that Parliament amends the Constitution by ensuring that a constitutional court preside and hears the disqualification petition against the members of the House. Any member who is disqualified under the Tenth schedule should be barred from contesting elections for at least 10 years from the date of order. Also, then his family members (namely father, mother, son, daughter) should be barred from contesting elections for the vacated seat.[17]

CHAPTER THIRTY-ONE

RECOVERY OF DEBT WITHOUT INTERVENTION OF COURTS

Author: Abhigyan, IV year of B.A.,LL.B. from Delhi Metropolitan Education, Noida Affiliated to GGSIPU, Delhi

Introduction

India's banking industry has played a critical role in the country's attempt to achieve fast economic growth but the road to this was not really easy and smooth. A bank performs various functions, out of which providing credit to the client is one of the primary and major function of the banks. However, credit is a fragile plant that thrives under favourable conditions but withers quickly amid adversity and it carries the seed of its own demise. As a result, when banks/financial institutions lend, theyfirst ensure that the loan is returned when due and, second, that it is utilised for authorised reasons.

However, loan recovery is one of the most challenging challenges that these institution address, regardless of whether the loan is short-term, medium-term, or long-term, or to whom the loan is given. The then existing legal framework relating to commercial transactions was not able to not keep up with evolving business practises and banking sector reforms. This resulted in a slow pace of recovery of defaulting loans which escalated the levels of non-performing assets of banks and financial institutions and were becoming a big hurdle to rapid development.

In this abstract we will have a look into the existing legal framework and process of Recovery of debt by banks and Financial Institutions without the intervention of court.

Existing Legal framework for Recovery of Debts

Indian legal system provides various legal provisions for the recovery of debts, these include:

1. Suit under CPC; Summary suits can be filed by the lender under Order XXXVII of the Code of Civil Procedure, 1908

2. Criminal complaint under Section 138 of NI Act,1881 (Negotiable Instruments Act) for dishonour of any cheque issued by borrower to the bank in discharge of legally enforceable liability.

3. Arbitration under the Arbitration & Conciliation Act, 1996 for the recovery of amount due as specified in the Arbitration Agreement /clause in the loan instruments, in circumstances where RDDBFI Act is inapplicable.

4. OA by Banks and FI's before the DRT for a loan above Rs. 20 lakhs, under RDDBFI ACT, 1993.

5. Enforcement of Security Interest under SARFAESI ACT, 2002

Out of the following measures, we will discuss the recovery of debts under the DRT Act and SARFAESI Act as it provides for the banks and FinancialInstitutions to proceed without the intervention of courts.

RDDBFI Act, 1993 ("Recover of Debts due to Banks and Financial Institutions")

Prior to ratification of the RDDBFI Act, banks and FI's faced significant difficulties in recovering debts from borrowers because the courts were overburdened with a large number of regular cases, preventing the courts from giving priority to bank and financial institution recovery matters.

"The Government of India formed a committee headed by Mr T. Tiwari in 1981, and this committee proposed a quasi-judicial setup exclusively for banks and financial institutions, which, by using a summary procedure, can quickly dispose-off recovery cases filed by banks and financial institutions against borrowers. In 1991, a committee chaired by Mr.Narasimham backed the Mr T. Tiwari Committee's findings and proposed the formation of quasi-judicial debt collection agencies to expedite debt recovery. As a result, the Government of India adopted the RDDBFI Act. Through the enactment of RDDBFI Act, quasi-judicial bodies, i.e., the DRT (Debt Recovery Tribunal) and DRAT (Debt Recovery Appellate Tribunal) were established, and a system for debt collection was established.

The first DRT was established in Calcutta on 27th April 1994."[i]Presently there are 39 DRT's and 5 DRAT in India.

Constitutionality of Act

The Act's constitutionality was contested in the case of "Union of India &Anr. vs. Delhi High Court Bar Association &Ors."[ii] The Act's constitutionality was challenged on the grounds that it was irrational, violated Article 14 of the Constitution, and exceeded the legislative competence of Parliament.

The Supreme Court ruled that "while Articles 323A and 323B specifically enable the legislature to enact laws for the establishment of tribunals, the power of the parliament to enact a law constituting a tribunal such as a banking tribunal is not taken away in relation to the matter specified therein." It was observed that, in exercising its legislative competence, the parliament can offer a mechanism for recovering payments owed to banks and financial institutions, therefore upholding the Act's legitimacy.

Pecuniary Jurisdiction

For any debts worth more thansum of Rs. 20 Lakhs, an application for the recovery of debt can be made to thetribunal. Banks and FI's can use the standard remedy and approach Civil Courts, for smaller sums.

Jurisdiction of Tribunal

Section 17 of the RDDBFI Act gives the tribunal jurisdiction, power, and authority to entertain and decide applications from secured creditors for recovery of debts owed to such secured creditors. The DRT and DRAT's jurisdictional powers and authority are structured in such a way that civil courts do not directly intervene on the principal issue on which DRTs must rule. Furthermore, section 17A gives DRAT overall superintendence and control, as well as appellate jurisdiction over DRT.

Section 18 of the Act prohibits all other Courts from hearing debt related matters, with the exception of the Supreme Court and High Court, whose power is derived from Articles 226 and 227 of the Indian Constitution. The basic line is that only the High Court and the Supreme Court may grant redress against a DRAT verdict.

While the DRT procedure was intended to relieve the burden on lower courts, the lower courts do play a part in the DRT process since the judicial powers placed on the DRT and DRAT under the RDDBFI Act are extremely limited. In the case of "Standard Chartered Bank vs. DharmindarBhoi and others"[iii], the Supreme Court emphasised in its decision that the DRT and DRAT can only adjudicate on topics within their scope as established in section 17 of this Act. For example, DRTs and DRATs do not have authority over property succession rights, monitoring and enforcing KYC rules, or issuing receipts.Thus, disputes on such topics necessitate decisions from civil courts, which have greater authority than DRTs and DRATs.

Application to Tribunal

Under section 19, "the bank or financial institution for the recovery of any debt can file an application to the tribunal within the local limits of whose jurisdiction:

a) The branch or any other office of the bank or financial institution is maintaining an account in which debt claimed is outstanding, for the time being; or

b) The defendant, or each of the defendants where there are more than one, at the time of making the application, actually and voluntarily resides, or carries on business, or personally works for gain; or

c) Any of the defendants, where there are more than one, at the time of making the application, actually and voluntarily resides, or carries on business, or personally works for gain; or

d) The cause of action, wholly or in part, arises"[iv]

Right to Appeal

Under Section 20, an appeal to the order of tribunal may lie to the appellate tribunal i.e, the DRAT by the aggrieved person within period of 30 days from date on which the copy of order made by the DRT is received by borrower. Such appeal shall only be entertained on the submission of 50% of amount of the debt by the borrower which can be reduced to 25% by the tribunal but cannot be waived.

SARFAESI Act, 2002("Securitisation and Reconstruction of Financial Assets and Enforcement of Security Interest")

Even after the RDDBFI Act was passed, issues such as a lack of liquidity, an asset-liability mismatch, and long-term asset blockage continued. Banks were unable to recover their dues to the level predicted even after the establishment of DRTs.

"To overcome those gaps, the federal government formed different committees, such as the Narasimham Committee I (1991) and the Narasimham Committee II (1998) and Andhyarujina Committee constituted under the chairmanship of Sri T.R. Andhyarujina, to investigate banking sector reforms. These committees evaluated the need for changes to the legal framework and the creation of new securitization legislation that permits banks and financial institutions to take control of assets and sell them without the need for judicial intervention. In the year Finally, the SARFAESI ACT was approved in 2002."[v]

Object of the Act

"The Securitisation and Reconstruction of Financial Assets and Enforcement of Security Interest Act, 2002", was enacted to regulatesecuritization and reconstruction of financial assets, as well as the enforcement of security interests created in favour of secured creditors.

The Act specifies three possible techniques for recovering NPAs:

a) Securitization

(b) Asset Reconstruction; and

(b) Enforcing security without the intervention of the court.

Constitutionality of Act

In the case of "Mardia Chemicals Ltd. Vs Union of India"[vi],constitutionality of SARFAESI was challenged, namely "Sections 13, 15, 17, and 34", on the grounds that they are excessive and arbitrary.The Supreme Court in its judgement upheld the constitutionality of SARFAESI.

Pecuniary Jurisdiction

"The provisions of SARFEASI Act applies to NPA loan accounts of value exceeding Rs. 1 Lakh and the NPA loan account is more than a twentieth of principle and interest. Such NPAs should be backed by securities charged to the banks by way of hypothecation, mortgage or assignment and the secured assets."[vii]

Recovery Process under SARFAESI

On the account of the borrowers failure of due payment of loan, bank declares the loan account as NPA andsend notice to the borrower under Section 13(2). On receiving such NPA notice from bank, the borrower has 60 days to discharge his liabilities. In case borrower fails to do so, the secured creditor proceeds under Section 13(4) of the Act for the enforcement of Security Interest.

"The secured creditor may take one or more recourse mentioned in under section 13(4) namely,

i. To take possession of the secured assets of the borrower including the right to transfer by way of lease, assignment or sale for releasing the secured asset. When it comes to taking possession of the property, there are two things like taking symbolic possession and taking actual possession

ii. To take over the management of the business of the borrower including the right to transfer by way of lease, assignment or sale for releasing the secured asset.

iii. Appoint the manager, to manage the secured asset whose possession has been taken

iv. Requiring money from any person who has acquired any of the secured assets from the borrower and from whom any money is due to the borrower, to pay to the secured creditor, by notice in writing"[viii]

The Secured creditor under Section 14 may request by writing to the jurisdictional Chief Metropolitan Magistrate or District Magistrate to take possession thereof. Such Magistrate may then take control of the asset and deliver it to the secured creditor. And may use or cause the use of such force as he deems necessary.

Remedy to Aggrieved Borrower

"Any individual who is aggrieved by any measure taken under section 13(4) by the secured creditor may file an application with the tribunal within 45 days of the date such measures were adopted under Section 17 of the Act. If the tribunal concludes, after reviewing, that the measures under section 13(4) are in violation of the Act, it may declare the measures invalid and return the borrower's possession of the secured asset."[ix]

Right to Appeal

Any Individual aggrieved by the order of DRT may approach the DRAT under Section 18 of the act provided that no appeal shall lie unless the borrower has deposited 50% of the amount of debt owed by the borrower.

RDDBFI and SARFAESI Complimentary

In the case of"Transcore Vs. UOI"[x], it was held that RDDBFI Act, 2016 and SARFAESI Act are complementary to each other. The withdrawal of an action pending before the tribunal under RDDBFI, 1993 is not a prerequisite for resorting to SARFAESI. The SARFAESI Act of 2002 is an extra remedy that is not inconsistent with the DRT Act of 1993, and hence the theory of election does not apply.

Conclusion

The rising NPAs and debt issues are hurting the banking industry and the economy as a whole and the enactment of new laws have provided a relief to both judiciary and secured creditors for the recovery of the same but it can be seen that no law dealing with the recovery of loans is complete in itself; for example, money recovery suit filed under CPC in the Civil Court takes long to be decided because of the already plethora of cases within courts, and laws dealing specifically with recovery suits, such as the RDDBFI Act 1993, are only competent to deal with unsecured loans; for secured loans, the remedy under it is inadequate. Similarly, proceedings under the SARFAESI Act, 2002 deals specifically with the secured loan, and there are numerous complications under the Act for obtaining possession without the intervention of the court. Also secured creditors are compelled to file application before the Chief Metropolitan Magistrate or District Magistrate for the possession of assets which is a time-consuming process. Thus, all of the aforementioned remedies are incomplete in themselves and reliant on each-other at various levels.

Author's Biography

A law student who is ambitious and has professional intellect with progressive legal experience gained through internships which have honed the pressure handling skills and working with deadlines. Expeditious writing skills and conversance with legal research work are strong suits. A keen learner always looking forward to the insightful experience and polishing present knowledge.

REMEDIES AVAILABLE WITH BORROWER OR AGGRIEVED PERSON UNDER SECTION 17 SARFAESI ACT, 2002

Author: Abhigyan, IV Year of B.A.,LL.B, from Delhi Metropolitan Education, GGSIPU.

Introduction

India's banking industry has played a critical role in the country's attempt to achieve fast economic growth but the road to this was not really easy and smooth. The then existing legal framework relating to commercial transactions was not able to not keep up with evolving business practises and banking sector reforms. This resulted in a slow pace of recovery of defaulting loans which escalated the levels of non-performing assets of banks and financial institutions and were becoming a big hurdle to rapid development.

To overcome the problem of Non-performing assets and faster recovery of defaulting loans, Asset Securitisation and Reconstruction comes to the picture. We may now have a brief intro to what Asset Securitisation is.

Asset Securitisation and Reconstruction

Whenever a bank provides a secured loan be it a car, house or property loan or any type of loan, the banks keep with themselves some assets as mortgage in case that when there is a default in loan, the same mortgage can be used by the bank to recover their money given as loan. In such cases, the bank creates a pool of all such securities kept by the bank and coverts them into marketable bonds and debentures which can be easily liquefied to create fresh money. This is called Asset Securitisation. The first structured Asset Securitisation was done in USA in 1970.

The crisis of 2008 was also a result of bad mortgages kept by the bank as a security against which bonds were liquidised. As a consequence, the financial structure collapsed causing economic crisis.

SARFAESI ACT, 2002

In India, prior to the enactment of SARFAESI, the mode of recovery was governed by the Recovery of Debts due to Banks and Financial Institutions Act, however there were many loopholes in the act of which the lawyers and borrowers took advantage. In order to fill those gaps, the central government established the various committees such as Narasimham Committee I (1991) and Narasimham Committee II (1998), to examine banking sector reforms.

These committees assessed the necessity for changes in the legal framework and form new securitization law that allows banks and financial entities to take possession of securities and sell them without the need for court action. Finally, in 2002, SARFAESI ACT was passed.

Two main portals, i.e. the Debts Recovery Tribunal (DRT) and The Debts Recovery Appellate Tribunal (DRAT) were formed which allows for the speedier and procedural way of recovery.

Section 17: Remedies available with borrower or aggrieved person

Section 13 of the SARFAESI act provides for the secured creditor to enforce the security in case the account of borrower has been declared NPA. The secured creditor (FI/ bank) is required to send a 60-day notice to the borrower seeking repayment of the debt and outlining the assets over which the secured creditor intends to exercise its security interest. If the borrower fails to discharge its obligations to secured creditors by the end of the 60-day notice period, the secured creditor has the right to enforce security interest over secured assets under section 13(4).

Section 17 of SARFAESI provides remedies to the borrower or aggrieved person by any of the measures taken by the secured creditor referred in section 13(4). We will know have a detailed look into section 17.

Section 17 reads as:

(1) "Any person (including borrower), aggrieved by any of the measures referred to in sub-section (4) of section 13 taken by the secured creditor or his authorised officer under this Chapter, 2[may make an application along with such fee, as may be prescribed,] to the Debts Recovery Tribunal having jurisdiction in the matter within forty-five days from the date on which such measure had been taken:

Provided that different fees may be prescribed for making the application by the borrower and the person other than the borrower.

Explanation. - For the removal of doubts, it is hereby declared that the communication of the reasons to the borrower by the secured creditor for not having accepted his representation or objection or the likely action of the secured creditor at the stage of communication of reasons to the borrower shall not entitle the person (including borrower) to make an application to the Debts Recovery Tribunal under this sub-section.

(1A) An application under sub-section (1) shall be filed before the Debts Recovery Tribunal

within the local limits of whose jurisdiction--

(a) the cause of action, wholly or in part, arises;

(b) where the secured asset is located; or

(c) the branch or any other office of a bank or financial institution is maintaining an account

in which debt claimed is outstanding for the time being."

Clause (1) states that any person aggrieved from the measures taken by secured creditor under section 13(4) can make an application in the DRT within 45 days of the date when such measure has been taken. A proviso has been included stating that different fees may be for the application from the borrower itself and a person other than the borrower making the application.

The explanation under clause (1) states that the borrower cannot make an application for the non-acceptance of the representation or objection by the secured creditor.

Clause (1A) states that

Section 17 further reads as:

(2)"The Debts Recovery Tribunal shall consider whether any of the measures referred to in sub-section (4) of section 13 taken by the secured creditor for enforcement of security are in accordance with the provisions of this Act and the rules made thereunder.

(3) If, the Debts Recovery Tribunal, after examining the facts and circumstances of the case and evidence produced by the parties, comes to the conclusion that any of the measures referred to in sub-section (4) of section 13, taken by the secured creditor are not in accordance with the provisions of this Act and the rules made thereunder, and require restoration of the management or restoration of possession, of the secured assets to the borrower or other aggrieved person, it may, by order, -

(a) declare the recourse to any one or more measures referred to in sub-section (4) of section 13 taken by the secured creditor as invalid; and

(b) restore the possession of secured assets or management of secured assets to the borrower or such other aggrieved person, who has made an application under sub-section (1), as the case may be; and

(c) pass such other direction as it may consider appropriate and necessary in relation to any of the recourse taken by the secured creditor under sub-section (4) of section 13."

Clause (2) states that the DRT shall examine whether the measure taken by the secured creditor under section 13(4) is in accordance with the provisions of the rule and under clause (3), if the DRT on the basis of facts and circumstances of the case and evidences so produced comes to a conclusion that such measures are not in accordance with the provisions of act, shall by order either declare the measure taken invalid; or restore the management or possession of secured asset of aggrieved person; or pass any such direction as the DRT may consider appropriate.

Section 17 further reads as:

(4) "If, the Debts Recovery Tribunal declares the recourse taken by a secured creditor under sub-section (4) of section 13, is in accordance with the provisions of this Act and the rules made thereunder, then, notwithstanding anything contained in any other law for the time being in force, the secured creditor shall be entitled to take recourse to one or more of the measures specified under sub-section (4) of section 13 to recover his secured debt.

(4A) Where-

(i) any person, in an application under sub-section (1), claims any tenancy or leasehold rights upon the secured asset, the Debt Recovery Tribunal, after examining the facts of the case and evidence produced by the parties in relation to such claims shall, for the purposes of enforcement of security interest, have the jurisdiction to examine whether lease or tenancy

(a) has expired or stood determined; or

(b) is contrary to section 65A of the Transfer of Property Act, 1882 (4 of

1882); or

(c) is contrary to terms of mortgage; or

(d) is created after the issuance of notice of default and demand by the Bank

under subsection (2) of section 13 of the Act; and

(ii) the Debt Recovery Tribunal is satisfied that tenancy right or leasehold rights claimed in secured asset falls under the sub-clause (a) or sub-clause (b) or sub-clause (c) or sub-clause (d) of clause (i), then notwithstanding anything to the contrary contained in any other law for the time being in force, the Debt Recovery Tribunal may pass such order as it deems fit in accordance with the provisions of this Act."

Clause (4) states that if DRT declares that measure taken by secured creditor under section 13(4) is in accordance with provision of act, the secured creditor can take recourse to one or more measure for enforcement of security.

Clause (4A) states that if any person claims any tenancy or leasehold rights over the secured asset, the DRT will examine such claim and determine is the tenancy or lease has expired; or is contrary to provisions of TPA; or is contrary to terms of mortgage; or is created after the creditor issued notice under section 13 and if the tenancy or lease rights falls in any such category the DRT may take appropriate action.

Section 17 further reads as:

(5) "Any application made under sub-section (1) shall be dealt with by the Debts Recovery Tribunal as expeditiously as possible and disposed of within sixty days from the date of such application:

(6) If the application is not disposed of by the Debts Recovery Tribunal within the period of four months as specified in sub-section (5), any part to the application may make an application, in such form as may be prescribed, to the Appellate Tribunal for directing the Debts Recovery Tribunal for expeditious disposal of the application pending before the Debts Recovery Tribunal and the Appellate Tribunal may, on such application, make an order for expeditious disposal of the pending application by the Debts Recovery Tribunal."

Clause (5) states that DRT should deal with any such application within 60 days of filing which can be extended to 4 months and if the application is not disposed of as specified, an application can be filed to DRAT to order the DRT for speedier disposal of application.

Conclusion

Thus, provisions of SARFAESI act not only empowers the bank but also gives fair trial to the borrowers by giving efficacious remedy so that they can take recourse under section 17 of challenging every action of the secured creditor.

Author's Biography

A law student who is ambitious and has professional intellect with progressive legal experience gained through internships which have honed the pressure handling skills and working with deadlines. Expeditious writing skills and conversance with legal research work are strong suits.

A keen learner always looking forward to the insightful experience and polishing present knowledge.

CHAPTER THIRTY-THREE

PIRACY ETHICAL OR UNETHICAL, A KANTIAN PERSPECTIVE

Author: Abhigyan, IV year of B.A.,LL.B, from Delhi Metropolitan Education, GGSIPU.

Introduction

Among all the technological advancements seen in the past decade, the internet and other digital forms of communication and publication have taken the biggest leap. The methods by which various sorts of information can be communicated have likewise changed dramatically. A movie or a song can now be accessed anywhere and anytime, you can read a book without actually having a book and all of this on a single device. It has become an indispensable part of our life and with the increase in digital media, user's ability to reproduce, distribute, remix, and otherwise make use of content is growing too. However, everything comes with a risk.

There are more than 4 billion people using internet and 600 million people use internet in India alone and almost every day we hear of a new virus that causes substantial risk to data or loss of confidential data in businesses and government institutions. Therefore, parallel to the rise of digital media and growth of related industries, Intellectual property rights (IPR) are becoming more vulnerable to infringement. On one hand where internet makes our life easier, it puts up the copyright world at greater threat. In this article we aim to look at the copyright and piracy world through the lenses of Kantian perspective.

<u>Copyright and Piracy</u>

Copyright as defined by Merriam Webster is an "exclusive legal right to reproduce, publish, sell, or distribute the matter and form of something such as a literary, musical, or artistic work". To be simply tell, a copyright is a mechanism that ensures that only the original creator has the right to create copies of his creation and prevent all others from making such copies. "The basic idea behind such protection is the premise that innovations require incentives. Copyright recognizes this need and gives it a legal sanction"

However, as the internet continues to grow, so will the number of people who engage in internet based piracy. "Piracy refers to the unauthorized duplication of copyrighted content that is then sold at substantially lower prices in the 'grey' market."

"The origin of copyright had a link with the invention of printing press by Gutenberg in the fifteenth century. With the easy multiplying facility made possible by the printing press, there was voluminous increase in the printing and distribution of books which, in turn, led to adoption of unfair practices such as unauthorized printing by competing printers. Though piracy was born by the end of the fifteenth century, it was only in 1710 the first law on copyright in the modern sense of the term came into existence in England. The law which was known as `Queen Anne's Statute' provided authors with the right to reprint their books for a certain number of years."

Computers and the Internet have made it simple and inexpensive to copy and distribute software. Where the high cost of coping and distribution efforts previously represented a barrier to pirated material, the internet and computers have made piracy a major issue.

Kantian ethics

Immanuel Kant (1724-1804), a German philosopher was an opponent of utilitarianism. His work significantly followed the ethics of the Deontological theory. "The name comes from the Greek word deon, meaning duty or obligation." "A Deontological theory of ethics is one which holds that at least some acts are morally obligatory regardless of their positive or negative consequences on human beings."

To be simply put it means that the rightness or wrongness of an action is not judged by the consequence of that action but that the action confirms with our duty or the obligation. Kant in his theory focuses on Good Will, and there are two elements to having a good will: 1. Action must confirm to the Moral Law and; 2. A person must choose the right action solely because it is the right thing to do and not perform an action because he fears punishment or hopes for a reward.

An imperative is simply a command. There are two types of imperatives according to Kant: hypothetical and categorical imperatives. According to him a hypothetical imperative is a moral obligation applicable only in order to achieve a fixed goal. He pointed out that, "most of the time, whether or not we ought to do something isn't really a moral choice – instead, it's just contingent on our desires." Like, if your desire is to get money, then you ought to get a job. Kant called these if-then statements, hypothetical imperatives. These imperatives are about prudence rather than morality.

However, Kant focused morality in terms of what he called Categorical Imperatives, these are commands that one must perform regardless of what their consequence would be. Kant put two tests in order to identify what actions fits with the moral law. These are:

1 "The universalizability principle: Act only according to that maxim which you can at the same time will that it should become a universal law without contradiction"

This simply means that before doing an action you should ask yourself would you be willing to allow everyone else to do the same. For ex. If a student wants to cheat for a test he did not study, he should ask himself if he wants to live in a world where everyone, everywhere would cheat if they had not studied for the test. And if in case you accept your action of cheating, you are universalizing the same.

In addition to this, another test that followed is:

2. "The Humanity Principle: Act so that you treat humanity, whether in your own person or in that of another, always as an end, and never as a mere means."

This means that every human has individual intrinsic value and is capable of formulating their own purposes and goals and we cannot reduce others to mere objects for fulfilling our needs. The worth and value of human beings comes solely from what they are and not from the utility they perform for someone else.

Now here using someone as "mere means" is different from using someone. Humans are not objects to be used as mere means but they must be treated as an "end-in-themselves". This could be understood by illustrations. For ex. If I am using a pen and it runs out of ink, I would throw it because it does not fulfill my purpose anymore. This means that pen is a mere mean for me to write. But on the other hand you are using this article written by me to get information and I am using various articles to write this information. Kant says, you and I and the person I am receiving information from are autonomous have our own purposes, views and desires.

Piracy from Kantian Perspective

We will now look at the ethics of piracy through direct engagement with Kantianism. From Kantian perspective, it becomes very clear that the action of piracy is unethical. If we look at the first test of categorical Imperative we will find that if we confirm with the piracy for our own desires, we will be universalizing the act that everyone can pirate and sell pirated objects. If such happens no one will be willing to watch their innovations being sold off unethically, they would lose money and will not be able to afford to make further original copies.

Further if we look at the other test of Categorical imperative, piracy would mean that one does not admire the original creator and his ideas and is just using him as a mere means to fulfill his own desires. Where the original creator has his own needs and goals that me must achieve from his creation, piracy would rob him of this and he would not be treated as Kant says an "end to himself"

Thus there is no doubt that from a Kantian perspective, the action of piracy is itself unethical, regardless of what the consequence of the action would be.

Conclusion

Piracy is an obvious issue that not only has a negative impact on individual but it also hampers local and national growth. The act today is so easy to carry and is as difficult to trace. The very base of piracy that one individual is benefitted is against the ethics of morality. It demotivates the original creators, decreases innovations ad violates the very right of copyright. Every state must take necessary steps to implement and modernize their intellectual property laws. Individual must be aware of their rights over their original creation and their right to make copies of it.

CHAPTER THIRTY-FOUR

FAST-TRACK ARBITRATION: A NOVEL SOLUTION TO INTERNATIONAL ARBITRAL DELAY

Author: Umra Rehmani, B.A.,LL.B(Hons.) From Faculty of Law, Aligarh Muslim University.

Co-author: Zoya Khan, B.A.,LL.B(Hons.) From Faculty of Law, Aligarh Muslim University.

Abstract

Almost all the activities have been halted by the noble coronavirus yet the legal arena has not failed to play its significant role as a peace maker. Alternate Dispute Resolution, in particular, Fast-Track Arbitration, is said to be one of the speedy resorts for settling down the disputes between the parties by getting the arbitral awards within months rather than years. Basically, fast track arbitration is not a distinct system of arbitration. But it is actually a general characterization for an accelerated arbitral procedure. It actually enables the parties to resolve their disputes mutually and with ease at their homes digitally. It is also well-known for its cost efficiency, quick disposal of disputes and rendering of international arbitral awards by avoiding unnecessary proceedings to be followed in the Courts.

Thus, Fast Track Arbitration is not just fast but it is actually efficaciously fast. The parties can opt it either before or at the time of the appointment of arbitral tribunal. Hence, the Parties looking for an efficient and speedy resolution of their disputes can definitely resort to Fast Track Arbitration. Though, the Parties cannot knock the doors of the Court to mandatory impose the process of Fast Track Arbitration upon them. This article outlines a brief as to why Fast-Track Arbitration should be encouraged world-wide? This paper uses qualitative approach to describe and discuss efficiency of Fast-Track Arbitration, also known as Expedited Arbitration.

Keywords: Arbitrator, Arbitral award, Cost-efficient, Dispute, Fast-track arbitration.

<u>INTRODUCTION</u>

The ever-increasing complex ties between firms, investors, and states have resulted from the rise and globalisation of cross-border investment and trade. Though such partnerships may ultimately fail and the parties must evaluate the best methods for resolving any issues that may emerge. Arbitration became the normal procedure for resolving disagreements in many circumstances. Hence, commercial arbitration is a private form of binding dispute resolution before an unprejudiced bench that arises from the parties' agreement but is regulated and executed by the state. Transnational commercial arbitration has not yet lived up to its eventuality as a medium of dispute resolution. Theoretically, Arbitration is a more expeditious means of resolving disputes than litigation in a judicial forum.

Though, internationally it is characterized by procedural delays. Thus, several solutions have been proposed to expedite transnational commercial arbitration, including an arbitral court of appeal, a one-time arbitrator system with obligatory primary meetings. Recently, fast-track international arbitration has come to rescue from the problem of arbitral delay.

The American Review of International Arbitration has also applied fast-track solution. Fast Track arbitration may be demarcated as a complete arbitration technique compressed into a shorter length for a quicker decision of the dispute. Parties may additionally opt this technique or not. After opting for it, an emergency provision is supplied for in maximum country wide arbitration acts and arbitration guidelines.

Fast-track arbitration shows a silver lightning as a mode of expediting international arbitral procedure. However, if it is to make fast-track arbitration a feasible volition alternative to conventional transnational arbitration, it must be institutionalized. It is therefore proposed that international arbitration institutions adopt optional fast-track arbitration rules to supplement their current rules of arbitration.

FAST TRACK ARBITRATION: AN INSIGHT

Foremost, it is significant to note that fast track arbitration is not a separate system of arbitration but relatively a general depiction for an accelerated and augmented arbitral procedure. Arbitral proceedings with very rigorous deadlines are usually referred to as fast-track arbitration. Expedited Arbitration is an operative mode of resolution which cannot be delayed due to any reason whatsoever. Being a part of normal arbitration, a sole Arbitral Tribunal is established upon the consent and accord of parties in it, having restricted procedures to be followed to accelerate the procedure of dispute resolution. Through Fast Track Arbitration, a swift and operative award is pronounced by the Arbitral Tribunal thus, cutting down the costs and adjournments allied with a regular arbitration. Fast track arbitration would be distinguished from emergency arbitration, that is also a compressed procedure permitting a party to apply for urgent interim or conservatory procedures that cannot anticipate the constitution of an arbitral tribunal. Such strategies, are opposite to an award issued below a fast-track arbitration, does now no longer have a res judicata effect.

Fast track arbitration is a kind of ad hoc arbitration. Numerous significant international arbitration institutions propose explicit rules for fast-track arbitration such as American Arbitration Association, the Arbitration Institute of the Stockholm Chamber of Commerce & the German Institute of Arbitration. Fast track arbitration may also take place under the rules of institutions which lack exact regulations for accelerated procedures, or have only undeveloped and basic provisions in this regard. The utmost well-known fast track arbitration cases to date were directed under the rules issued by the International Chamber of Commerce. Even though Article 32 of the ICC Rules commonly offers for expedited procedures by conceding the parties the chance to shorten various time limits set out in these rules, the ICC Rules do not comprehend supplementary exhaustive procedures in this regard. Moreover, parties may move themselves onto a "fast track" by postulating particular time limits for each phase of an ad-hoc proceeding, or by stipulating a deadline for any award, either in the arbitration clause or in a later agreement.

VARIOUS FACETS OF A FAST-TRACK ARBITRATION

Fast track arbitration is made up of a defined set of pieces, it comprises a variety of expedited methods. However, there are a number of procedural options that, when used in various combinations, create recognised parts of fast-track arbitrations.

1. It is primarily governed by strict time-limit policies that must be followed by both the arbitrators and the parties. This simply means expediting the arbitral process and resolving the dispute in the shortest period possible.
2. Any activity that aids in the determination of the issue as quickly as possible is accepted under fast-track arbitration. It does not include a fixed collection of elements or procedures to be followed as per ordinary arbitral proceedings.
3. Fast Track Arbitration Procedures frequently do not require oral hearings and rely solely on written submissions.
4. The parties may choose a single arbitrator, and the submissions must be written in significant part by the parties themselves.
5. It defends the cost, speed, and time without violating any laws, and it frequently prevents procedures such as witness interviews.

Strict time restrictions are the most important aspect of a fast-track arbitration. These deadlines apply to both the parties and the arbitrators. Parties are typically held to tight deadlines for their respective arbitrator's recommendation, as well as their filings and preparation for the oral hearing. Meanwhile, the arbitrator's most significant constraint is a deadline for issuing the award. The minimization of procedural steps is another important feature of a fast-track arbitration. As a result, the most stringent limits on expedited proceedings include constraints on the number of written submissions as well as hearing limitations. Furthermore, without modern communication tools, a fast-track arbitration is unlikely. Communication by email, fax, phone, and video conferences, as well as any other relevant ways of minimising superfluous formality, is a vital aspect in the fast-track arbitration hearings' significantly reduced duration.

FUNDAMENTALS OF FAST TRACK-ARBITRATION

Apart from the two most essential aspects of arbitration, speed and cost effectiveness, there are a number of elements of arbitration, as well as fast-track arbitration, that make it a viable option to state jurisdiction. Those fundamentals include;

1. Independence of the parties
2. Equity of treatment
3. Impartiality and Independence of an Arbitrator and
4. Enforcement of arbitral awards

- **Independence of the parties**

This Arbitration provides the flexibility to the parties in choosing the framework for resolving their dispute based on the facts of the case. The parties are free to choose arbitration as a method of conflict resolution and to create the rules that govern it—from the location of the arbitration and the applicable (substantive and procedural) law to the number of arbitrators and the specifics of the proceedings. It is also a matter of party autonomy whether or not to commit to fast-track arbitration.

Arbitrators may only disregard the parties' choice of substantive and procedural law relevant to the arbitration in only restricted and highly exceptional circumstances. In international arbitration, the arbitrator's decision is guided by the application of transnational principles of private international law, and there is a growing trend toward applying substantive transnational law principles directly to the merits of a case in order to designate the applicable rules of law. The arbitrator's ability to pick the appropriate legislation is essentially limited only by international public policy principles. Under the jura novit curia rule, the judge or arbitrator is expected to actively explore the appropriate foreign law while determining the relevant norms of law in most civil law jurisdictions. Furthermore, foreign law is viewed as a question of fact in common law jurisdictions.

Furthermore, in arbitral processes where the parties anticipate the arbitrator to actively research the law, the parties or the appointing body may be well advised to select an arbitrator with a thorough understanding of the applicable national law. The relevant contents of the applicable law are more likely to be determined in fast-track arbitration based on the submissions of the parties alleging a claim under a specific national law.

In fast-track arbitrations, the rules guiding the proceedings can be established in an arbitration agreement or arbitration clause, or the parties can agree to a set of institutional norms at any point before the arbitration begins. In the absence of enforceable guidance from the parties or applicable institutional standards, the arbitrator has the right—and the obligation—to determine the arbitration rules as he or she sees appropriate. International arbitration institutions have been a helpful source of guidance for arbitrators when it comes to accepting evidence in this regard. While international arbitral tribunals are generally free to admit evidence at their discretion, they must adhere to basic principles of fairness in order for the resulting award to be enforceable.

The decision to use fast-track arbitration will not necessarily be without repercussions in terms of the procedural norms, and hence may have a significant impact on the fact-finding process. Limitations may, however, apply not only to hearings, but also to the categories of evidence accepted in fast-track arbitrations. Also, in fast-track processes, there may be circumstances where the arbitrator directly or tacitly decreases the amount of proof required, or otherwise lessens the plaintiff's burden of proof (by taking into account the limits indicated above).

- **Equity of Treatment**

While fast track arbitration has procedural limits, these limitations must not detract from the parties' equal treatment. It would be a mistake to presume that the parties who consented to fast-track arbitration also agreed to have their procedural rights limited. The notion of giving each party a reasonable amount of time to make their case is both basic and obligatory. As a result, under the fast-track arbitration, due process and procedural fairness are two features of equitable treatment.

The extent to which due process rights are observed in a fast-track arbitration is largely determined by the facts of the case. For example, the parties' pleadings should be made available to their opponents early enough to allow them to respond; arbitrator orders regarding future procedures or deadline extensions in favour of one party should be communicated promptly; and the parties should be given an equal opportunity to comment on proffered evidence. Of course, the parties' choice of an accelerated dispute resolution procedure must be taken into account when determining what constitutes "adequate time" in a fast-track arbitration.

The time constraints established in accelerated processes also diminish the amount of time the arbitrator has to make a decision. However, because of the unique nature of accelerated procedures, it is not commonplace to forego the necessity of a reasoned award in order to save even more time. When it comes to procedural fairness, it is sometimes characterised in subjective terms and reflects a party's position in a certain case. In most fast-track cases, however, it will not be unreasonable to refuse multiple days of hearings, a large number of witnesses, or extensive arguments in order to save time and money. Nonetheless, it is critical to guarantee that each party has enough time to react properly to its opponent's evidentiary presentations. Even in circumstances when fast-track arbitration is a feasible means of dispute settlement, a state court's support for the implementation of such an award requires adherence to a minimal degree of due process.

- **Arbitrator's independence**

An impartiality as well as independence arbitrator is the core element of the fast-track arbitration. The achievement of the aim of such arbitration proceedings will depend on the arbitrator's ability to make the assessment of the parties through an unbiased and systematic procedure. At first, the parties should mutually appoint an independent arbitrator for avoiding the difficulty in appointing an alternative arbitrator in case of arbitrariness due to the available time restrictions.

- **Enforceability**

The decisions made in fast-track proceeding is only valuable when its enforceability is ensured. The expeditious disposal of a dispute offers several benefits to the parties. Thus, arbitrators in fast-track arbitration must bind themselves by the above-mentioned fundamentals to ensure that the award rendered can be easily enforced. But the failure to comply with these fundamentals may cause an arbitral award to be set aside under the applicable national law or may otherwise constitute a ground for the refusal of award enforcement.

The enforcement of a fast-track arbitral award is generally governed by the Convention on the Recognition and Enforcement of Foreign Arbitral Awards. It is commonly known as the New York Convention 1958. The grounds for refusal of a fast-track arbitral award are provided in Article V of the New York Convention. While Section 1(b) deals with the violation of due process rights, and section 2(b) deals with the public policy issues.

Under International law, the violations of procedural rights as grounds for refusing to recognize and enforce an arbitral award is not generally pleaded before the state courts. The recognition and enforcement of an arbitral award which may be denied at the request of the party against whom it is invoked if the party claiming it was unable to prove his case. Further, Article V, Section 1(b) of the New York Convention provides that the identified violation had a direct influence on the outcome of the arbitral proceedings.

The following procedural defects are considered as grounds for violation of procedural rights by the state courts:

1. failure to inform a party of the opposing party's arguments
2. failure to present substantial document by one party that are submitted to the arbitrator by the other party, and
3. the subsequent denial of the opportunity given to comment thereupon
4. the subsequent denial of the opportunity to comment on expert written reports or oral statements.

The State courts don't consider limitation of the deadline for submissions made by the arbitrator as a ground of violation of procedural rights. The arbitrator can direct that a decision was to be made by a certain date and based on the documents made available up until that date basing an award on certain select arguments rather than all arguments set forth by a party during the proceedings. The enforceability of an arbitral award becomes a bit difficult due to the implicit time limits. Thus, the utmost care is to be given in ensuring that all submissions by one party in the proceedings are presented to the other party.

ARBITRAL AWARDS AGAINST THE PUBLIC POLICY

The State Courts may refuse the enforcement of arbitral award if such recognition and enforcement of the award would be contrary to the public policy of that country. The recognition and enforcement of an arbitral award can also be refused if it is given in violation of a legal norm which constitutes the public policy of the State. It can also be rejected by the State Courts if the arbitral award intolerably contradicts the general principles of justice and equity. However, Article V, Section 2(b) of the New York Convention is rarely being invoked by state courts as a ground for refusal of enforcement.

The consideration of a procedural defect to be against the public policy, necessarily need not to be backed by the legal confirmation. Such recognition and enforcement of the arbitral award must also be intolerable for the domestic legal system itself. Thus, the State Courts consider international arbitral awards to be contrary to public policy of the state for the reasons stated above given under Article V, Section 1(b) of the New York Convention. When the parties had no equal opportunity to comment on an expert report during the arbitration proceedings, it can be treated as a ground of procedural defect against the public policy. Further, rendering of comparatively less reasonable arbitral award by a State Court is not a sufficient ground to refuse recognition and enforcement of an arbitral award in the state where the enforcement was sought did not set out the requirement of a reasoned award.Though, the parties to arbitration should generally claim for a reasonable arbitral award as a prerequisite for enforcement of it by the State Courts.

UTILITY OF FAST-TRACK ARBITRATION

Fast-track arbitration is well-known for ensuring a super-quick resolution of the dispute between the parties. As a result, receiving an award within weeks or three to six months of the start of the proceedings is far faster than a typical or traditional arbitration process. Though the above-mentioned merit can only be accomplished via better collaboration between the parties. With their disciplined efforts of systematic written pleadings, both the parties and the arbitrators can make the arbitration more effective and time-efficient.

An issue concerning the arbitral the paint of Formula One racing vehicles came up before the arbitral tribunal in one of the most prominent cases of Formula One racing under the ICC Rules. In this case, both parties cooperated fully in the arbitration procedure. The parties did, in fact, exchange submissions at seven-day intervals. Thus, the arbitral tribunal also formulated its arbitral award within 48 hours of the hearing.

The concentration of material questions and evidence is another significant benefit of fast-track arbitration. As a result, exchanging lengthy briefs, holding protracted pleadings, or emphasising lengthy arguments is strongly discouraged. As a result, both the arbitrators and the parties must use their minds wisely in order to craft sharp arguments for the hearing. However, in a well-organized fast track arbitration case, there may be little opportunities for delay. However, the time restriction might be extended by the parties themselves if they agree. As a result, fast track arbitration leads to a quick and agreeable conclusion. Though it is unlikely to work in every contentious arbitration case.

Furthermore, if the fast-track proceedings are properly structured, they may result in increased party autonomy. As a result, the parties have complete control over the course and duration of the proceedings in order to achieve their long-term goals through fast-track arbitration.

However, the reality is that many parties do not choose fast track arbitration as their first option. When a party is too tired or reluctant to study the specific rules or processes in the event of a dispute, they often insert an arbitration clause.

Furthermore, parties can exert more control over the course of fast-track processes. Similarly, the right to be heard or the issue of due process may be influenced by the parties' actions. Interim measures are not required under the fast-track arbitration. This is because the arbitration must be completed quickly, and interim awards are frequently appealed, leading to a web-series number of cases. As a result, a fast-track arbitration ruling is a conclusion in and of itself, requiring no further legal action. Interim awards are likely to provoke a legal challenge, effectively undermining the fast-track process. As a result of the lack of oral hearings, fewer submissions, this method becomes more efficient for both the parties. Fast track arbitration, on the other hand, may not be as cost-effective as it appears if it is not handled with care.

EFFICIENCY OF THE FAST-TRACK ARBITRATION DURING THE PANDEMIC

Fast track arbitration, as an alternative dispute resolution method, has changed the dynamics of commercial dispute settlement and is preferred by parties for several reasons, including the flexibility to determine procedures, fixed time restrictions, cost efficiency, and confidentiality, among others. Covid-19 has disrupted typical court procedures, forcing practitioners to seek for other, more efficient methods of resolving disputes. Parties who previously refused to consent to arbitration are increasingly accepting to settle their issues through mediation or arbitration.

Fast track arbitration looks to have higher assimilation skills with technology when compared to traditional litigation, owing to intrinsic party autonomy and freedom in deciding the leading procedures. When this tech-integration capability is considered, it is clear that the adoption and continuous reliance on arbitration as an alternative and effective means of dispute resolution has increased. Covid-19 and the resulting social-distancing measures have compelled disputing parties to implement and conduct arbitration proceedings remotely. Under normal circumstances, in-person hearings establish the general rule; but, because to Covid-19, this is currently not possible. As a result, typical courts and other judicial and quasi-judicial venues are increasingly relying on video-conferencing platforms to resolve ongoing cases. While it is encouraging to see the long-overdue shift toward the use of technology in conflict resolution, there are several problems and issues that continue to stymie this necessary transformation. When compared to pre-Covid-19 times, Covid-19 has increased the regularity of virtual arbitrations. It would also be a practical solution for litigants seeking redress during the COVID – 19 pandemics, when courts are unable to conduct normal hearings and are overburdened by the pending litigation of several cases.

CONCLUSION

Fast Track Arbitration is legally proven to be way efficient resort rather than just fast modern hack of dispute resolution. We live in the techno-world where every second has its value and even one minute wasted is a lost for a business. Thus, Fast Track Arbitration can lead the way through and create a path for technologically-savvy modes of resolving disputes. Fast Track proceeding is the one of the best methods to be opt for speedy disposal of the disputes. It subsequently cut downs the case costs and also, helps in maintaining amicable relations between the parties. Though the future of fast track proceeding greatly depends upon the cooperation of the parties and the arbitrator as well. Though, Fast Track arbitration should be preferred when the quantum of dispute is smaller compared to cost of dispute resolution

Nowadays, the parties tend to submit voluminous documents with attachments to the arbitrators far in excess of the amount of material they would produce before the court of law. Also, the parties tend to make repeated requests for time extensions in a strategic effort to delay the proceedings. But such efforts are just a throw of an arrow in the dark that paves unnecessary delay for a decision of the case.

Thereby, it is a high time to do away with the Court formalities, physical hearings or unnecessary procedural ceremonies to dispose of no. of ever-pending cases of arbitration. So, fast track proceedings must be encouraged by both the disputed parties and the arbitral tribunal. If the Fast-track proceedings are organised professionally by all participants involved, there cannot be any reason to considered it as a less efficient and fair dispute settlement procedure. Therefore, there is a general and collective urge to encourage the fast-track arbitration throughout the globe in these times of crisis.

Authors' Biography

Umra Rehmani and Zoya Khan, both are the Final year students, currently pursuing B.A.LL.B (Hons.) from the Faculty of Law, Aligarh Muslim University, Aligarh. Being a legal enthusiast both the authors are highly motivated to bring about a refreshing change through their knowledge, experience and skills to achieve their goals.

CHAPTER THIRTY-FIVE

DOMESTIC VIOLENCE AGAINST WOMEN

Author: Amisha Mathur, II Year of B.A.,LL.B from Ajeenkya DY Patil University, Pune.

Talking for the repression of violence is a symbol of evolution. The United Nations defines violence against women as "any act of gender-based violence that results in, or is likely to result in, physical, sexual, or mental harm or suffering to women, including threats of such acts, coercion or arbitrary deprivation of liberty, whether occurring in public or in private life."(1).

The practice of domestic violence is very common in many countries including India. The practice of domestic violence is present not only at the global level but also present in every aspect of society. It was found that worldwide, nearly 1 in 3, or 30%, of women, have been subjected to physical and/or sexual violence by an intimate partner or non-partner sexual violence or both. (2).

Domestic violence put a serious impact on women's health and well-being. Women can suffer from domestic violence anywhere, at home, the workplace, in public spaces, and even on online platforms also. Violence against women and girls can be committed by anyone, it can be committed by their family members, intimate partners, friends, employers, community members, state and even by government also etc.

There is no single or uniform reason that leads to domestic violence. Types of domestic violence include Physical abuse which includes assault, criminal force, and criminal intimidation are forms of physical abuse that can range from normal slapping to even can cause the death of a person.

Emotional abuse consists of yelling, blaming, and controlling behaviour are also forms of emotional abuse. Economic abuse, controlling victim through financial resources. There is no single or uniform reason that leads to domestic violence. It's a combination of various reasons and factors that present in society that leads to domestic violence like the demand for dowery which is still in practice mostly in India (3), cultural factors such as the desire for a male child, religious factors such as still having thinking that just because she is having mensuration, she is impure, male-dominated society, lack of education system and many mostly these are all major factors that can lead to domestic violence against women. The practice of domestic violence can put serious impacts on victims such as they can suffer from emotional and psychological trauma, economic homelessness, financial effects, and can affect or put negative impacts on children and their behaviour. It can also lead to death, illness, injury, and disability.

When we talk about protection from domestic violence, more than one billion women around the world live in places that afford them almost zero protection against domestic sexual violence (4). It's quite a disturbing fact that more than 600 million women live in nations with no laws protecting them against domestic violence in general. The highest concentration of these nations is located in regions in the Middle East, Western Asia, and sub-Saharan Africa. There are different types of law in different countries but there are still 46 countries where women do not have any legal protection against domestic violence and there are a total of 15 countries where domestic violence is legal such as Niger, Pakistan, Lesotho, Latvia, Yemen and many. Here are some laws related to domestic violence by different countries, in India, The Protection of Women from Domestic Violence Act, 2005 is a civil law that ensures the protection of not just married women against men, but also women who are in live-in relationships, as well as family members including mothers, grandmothers, etc.

Under this law, women can pursue violence, abuse, battery and can even further claim financial compensation and the right to live in their shared household. She can even ask for maintenance from her abuser in case they are living apart. This law assures women do not get kicked out of their own homes and are able to sustain themselves in case they have faced violence. A Magistrate can also pass a protection order to ensure that the abuser does not contact or is in close proximity survivor. When we specifically talk about Asia, most countries in Asia have laws against domestic violence, but nearly all laws exclude unmarried intimate partners, and half of the countries that have domestic violence laws do not include protections against economic violence which is one type of domestic as we discussed earlier. Globally, only one out of three countries protect unmarried intimate partners from domestic violence. Across all over Asia, most laws do not protect unmarried partners. Eighty-eight percent of women in the East Asia and the Pacific and 100 percent in South Asia are not protected against domestic violence by an unmarried intimate partner (5).

The conditions of rural areas regarding this practice are worst, victims don't know how to take any actions, they don't know any laws related to this practice because of a Limited awareness, capacity, and lack of political will that are the main reasons why women are behind in taking any actions regarding this practice mostly in rural areas. Although there are many campaigns and programs are started by the government to promote awareness but still, they have not accomplished actual targets.

So overall we can see domestic violence, which is a very common practice in the world, and currently, we can say many women are suffering from this problem, there are many factors that led to domestic violence as we discussed above, the main factor that contributes to this practice is lack of awareness among peoples regarding this practice, creating awareness is very important especially among women. Although there are many campaigns and programs are started by the government to promote awareness but still, they have not accomplished actual targets.

It's important to talk about it openly on public platforms, if we see or we came to know about any such woman suffering from this practice, we should inform the police and try her to get justice. We should try to teach girls about domestic violence and how to take action against it. The government of the country should implement more acts and legislation related to this practice.

<u>Author's Biography</u>

Amisha is a student at the school of law, Ajeenkya Dy Patil University Pune, pursuing BA LLB (Hons). She is a freelance writer and a blogger. Her main interest lies in writing about social issues in society and about legal topics. She has knowledge about contract law, intellectual property rights, and constitutional law. After pursuing her degree, she will be interested in working for a corporate firm

CHAPTER THIRTY-SIX

MARRIAGE RIGHTS OF THE LGBTQAI+ COMMUNITY IN INDIA

Author: Tanish Singh, III year of B.A.,LL.B from Symbiosis Law School, Hyderabad.

HISTORY OF THE LGBTQAI+ COMMUNITY IN INDIA

Records in ancient India –

Homosexuality has an antiquated history in India. Old writings like Rig-Veda which goes back around 1500 BC and figures and remnants delineate sexual acts between ladies as disclosures of a feminine reality where sexuality depended on joy and ripeness. The portrayal of gay acts in the Kamasutra, the Harems of youthful males kept by Muslim Nawabs and Hindu Aristocrats, male homosexuality in the Medieval Muslim history, confirmations of homosexuality in the Tantric customs are some chronicled confirmations of same-sex connections.

Reasons for the loss of LGBTQAI+ community's importance and punishments for homosexual behaviour in ancient India

Notwithstanding, these encounters began losing their importance with the emergence of Vedic Brahmanism and, later on, of British Colonialism. Giti claims that the Aryan invasion dating to 1500 B.C started to stifle homosexuality through the rising predominance of a male-controlled society. In the Manu smriti there are references to disciplines like loss of caste, overwhelming money-related fines, and strokes of the whip for gay and lesbian conduct. On account of wedded ladies, it is referenced that 'baiting of house cleaners' is to be rebuffed by shaving the ladies bare, cutting off two fingers and afterward strutting her on an ass. Manu's details of increasingly extreme disciplines for wedded ladies can propose either a wide pervasiveness of such connections among wedded ladies or a more prominent acknowledgment of these practices among unmarried ladies.

In either case, these references point to the strains in the standards of obligatory heterosexuality recommended by Brahmanical partite. Both sexual frameworks existed together, regardless of vacillations in relative restraint and opportunity, until British Colonialism when the devastation of pictures of gay expression and sexual expression by and large turned out to be progressively orderly and blatant.

Advent of British rule and its impact

The homophobic and Victorian strict qualities regarded the showcase of bold sexual pictures as obscene and fiendish. The Western view, since the hour of Colonial expansion, has been emphatically impacted by regenerative suspicion about sexuality. These strict qualities and mentalities were thus mapped into the translation of sexual activity among colonial people which is apparent from their reactions to all types of unnatural sexual practices. The Indian mind accepted the Western good and moral thought of sexuality being pathological as opposed to the natural articulation desire, which once used to be an intrinsic piece of Indian culture.

Changes in the notion of homosexuality in the last century

The last century saw significant changes in the notion of homosexuality. Since 1974, homosexuality stopped being viewed as strange conduct and was expelled from the classification of mental disorder. It was additionally de-condemned in various nations. From that point forward different states over the globe instituted against prejudicial or equivalent open-door laws and strategies to ensure the privileges of gays and lesbians. In 1994, South Africa turned into the principal country to constitutionally protect the privileges of lesbians and gays. Canada, France, Luxembourg, Holland, Slovenia, Spain, Norway, Denmark, Sweden, and New Zealand additionally have comparative laws. In 1996, the US Supreme Court requested that no state could pass enactment that oppressed gay people. In India, other than a few cases that provide the bare minimum like the National Legal Services Authority v. Union of India which resulted in the recognition of transgender people as a third gender other than that there have been a few cases but overall so far no such dynamic changes have occurred and the gay people remain victims of brutality in various structures bolstered by the state and society.

<u>WHAT IS LGBTQAI+ MARRIAGE?</u>

Definition of same sex marriage

Same-sex marriage or gay marriage is a union of two individuals of similar sex or sexual orientation, commenced in a civil or religious ceremony. The entire idea of gay marriage is to build up to marriage equity, which has contrasted and differed by jurisdiction. It has gone through an entire authoritative system of changes in court decisions including marriage laws. The progressions that are in discussion depend on the established assurances of acknowledgment and balance which the current marriage laws will permit. There are records of same-sex marriage going back to the 1ˢᵗ century. In the modern period, same-sex marriage began being legitimized toward the start of the 21ˢᵗ century. Today, it is accessible in 28 nations. Moreover, Taiwan and Costa Rica are additionally going to sanction same-sex marriage.

Countries where it is recognised and/or performed

Same-sex marriage is legitimately performed and recognized (across the country or in certain jurisdictions) in Argentina, Australia, Austria, Belgium, Brazil, Canada, Colombia, Denmark, Ecuador, Finland, France, Germany, Iceland, Ireland, Luxembourg, Malta, Mexico, the Netherlands, New Zealand, Norway, Portugal, South Africa, Spain, Sweden, Taiwan, the United Kingdom, the United States, and Uruguay. Same-sex marriage is additionally due to get legitimized in Costa Rica.

Israel recognizes same-sex relationships entered into abroad, as full relationships. Moreover, the Inter-American Court of Human Rights has given a judgment that is required to facilitate recognition in a few nations in the Americas. It is relevant to refer here that in the wake of leading an investigation in the United States from the year 1999 to 2015, there was a huge decrease in the complete pace of suicides after the introduction of same-sex marriage. The acknowledgment of gay marriage is both a civil and human right. it can be even said that the most prominent supporters of gay marriage are the Civil and Human Rights organization.

The introduction of same-sex marriage (likewise called marriage equality) has shifted by locale, and happened through legislative change to marriage law, court decisions dependent on constitutional assurances of equality, the acknowledgment that it is permitted by existing marriage law, or by direct popular vote (using referendums and initiatives).

The acknowledgment of same-sex marriage is viewed as a human right and a civil right just as a political, social, and strict issue. The most unmistakable supporters of same-sex marriage are human rights and social equality organizations as well as the clinical and scientific communities, while the most prominent rivals are strict religious gatherings. Surveys reliably show persistently rising help for the recognition of same-sex marriage in all developed democracies and some developing nations.

Impact of gay marriage

Scientific investigations show that the monetary, mental, and physical well-being of gay individuals are improved by marriage and that the offspring of same-sex guardians' profit by being raised by wedded same-sex couples inside a marital union that is recognized by law and bolstered by cultural institutions. Social science research demonstrates that the rejection of gay people from marriage derides and welcomes open victimization against them, with research additionally denying the idea that society relies solely on the union between heterosexuals.

Same-sex marriage can give those in committed same-sex relationships with appropriate government services and make financial demands on them practically identical to that required of those in inverse sex relationships, and furthermore gives them legal protections, for example, inheritance and other rights. Popular opinions opposing homosexual marriages are that homosexuality is unnatural and unusual, that the acknowledgment of same-sex associations will advance homosexuality in the public arena, and that kids are in an ideal situation when raised by inverse sex couples. These cases are disproved by logical examinations, which show that homosexuality is a characteristic and typical variety in human sexuality, and that sexual orientation is certainly not a conscious decision. Numerous examinations have indicated that offspring of same-sex couples toll similarly just as the offspring of inverse sex couples; a few investigations have demonstrated advantages to being raised by same-sex couples.

An investigation across the country information from over the United States from January 1999 to December 2015 uncovered that the foundation of same-sex marriage is related with a noteworthy decrease in the pace of attempted suicide among kids, with the impact being concentrated among offspring of a minority sexual direction, coming about in around 134,000 fewer kids attempting suicide every year in the United States.

<u>**What are the sections preventing/prohibiting it?**</u>

The law of our land doesn't give a similar set of rights and duties to the LGBTQIA+ couples that it does to hetero wedded couples. To quote Aditya Bondyopadhyay a Delhi-based lawyer and a veteran gay rights activist -

"Such a law isn't there in India. There are two aspects of marriage. One is the social aspect in which two consenting adults decide to go through a ritual in the presence (or not) of friends and family and treat his or her partner as a spouse. In India, post the Supreme Court verdict to decriminalise Section 377 of the Indian Penal Code, many can openly do that. However, there is a legal aspect of marriage that bestows rights and responsibilities on two people. These include, for example, property inheritance, maintenance of the spouse and so on. In heterosexual marriages, such rights and responsibilities come in a package. While an LGBTQIA+ couple can independently address such problems, there is no law in our country that can ensure their access to these rights. If you read our Special Marriage Act carefully, you will see it is meant for heterosexual couples. It doesn't even take into account transgender people."

Names/titles of laws prohibiting it

India doesn't recognize same-sex marriage or civil associations. Also, it doesn't have a concise clear and unified marriage law. Each Indian citizen has the privilege to pick which civil code will apply to them dependent on their community or religion. The following constitute India's marriage laws:"

- Indian Christian Marriage Act, 1872
- Special Marriage Act, 1954
- Hindu Marriage Act, 1955
- Parsi Marriage and Divorce Act, 1936
- Anand Marriage Act, 1909
- Muslim Personal Law (Shariat) Application Act, 1937

None of these legislated marriage acts unequivocally characterizes marriage as between a man and a lady. Neither do these legislations expressly restrict same-sex unions. However, the laws have "heteronormative underpinnings" and have been construed not to recognise same-sex unions.

Details of the uniform civil code proposed in 2017

Goa is the sole Indian state to have uniform marriage law. Each resident is bound to the uniform law, irrespective of their religion. However, Goa's Uniform Civil Code expressly characterizes marriage as being between individuals from the contrary sex.

Initiated in 2017, a draft of a Uniform Civil Code that would authorize same-sex marriage across the country has been proposed. [][] It addressed all the issues that this paper attempts to address and also additional issues.

It addresses the issue of marriage, which is defined as-

"the legal union as prescribed under this Act of a man with a woman, a man with another man, a woman with another woman a transgender with another transgender or a transgender with a man or a woman".

The issue of partnership and adoption Partnership has been defined as

"living together of a man with a woman, a man with another man, a woman with another woman a transgender with another transgender or a transgender with a man or a woman."

"It also provides that any two person who have been in partnership for more than two years shall have same rights and obligations towards each other as a married couple"

On the issue of adoption

"All married couple and couples in partnership entitled to adopt a child. Sexual orientation of the married couple or the partners not to be a bar to their right to adoption. "Non-heterosexual couples will be equally entitled to adopt a child"

Then the issues or religion and estate etc. are also addressed.

This is what was said by one Keshav Suri

"Marriage equality is one of the most basic rights for a citizen and the LGBTQ+ community is still devoid of it. I was lucky that my husband is French and we could marry in France, where it is legal. But there are millions who cannot. My foundation is working towards skilling and mainstreaming people from the community. We are also getting equipped to fight for marriage equality"

Marriage equity is one of the most fundamental rights for a citizen and the LGBTQAI+ people still lack those rights. In spite of the fact that perusing down of section 377 was notable, we have only just begun to scratch the surface, marriage is as yet a fantastical dream. There have been instances where lower courts of India have granted security to some same-sex couples [][][][]. We need to move in the direction of building a more approachable and holistic culture.

While organizations are talking of support, it is the ideal opportunity for positive/constructive efforts for the LGBTQAI+ people in society from every individual. The time has come to give the LGBTQAI+ people equivalent rights – marriage equality, work opportunities for us to have the option to carry on with a life of dignity.

Conclusion

Based all in all conversation on the part of same-sex marriage that is should it be authorized or not. This is more of a religious discussion than a political one. In which the researcher has given his contentions for decriminalizing it, I at long last close by saying that homosexuality isn't an offense, it is only a path for the quest for love, an approach to accomplish sexual want or desire. The researcher is of the opinion that there exists no rational argument that can justify criminalizing homosexuality, aside from personal bigotry, which restricts the people belonging to the LGBTQA+ community from enjoying the rights and protections which hetero couples enjoy. Marriage is a symbol of duty and love. If two men or two women desire to express that love and dedication, how does that decimate or harm the goals of marriage? Isn't India expected to be the place where there is freedom and tolerance? Homosexuality isn't new nor is it against the Indian culture, it has consistently existed and with lesser indictment.

What ought to be the correct way to deal with or manage same-sex relationships, the issues are very immense and complex. There is a developing conviction that our present strategy for condemning a same-sex sexual act neither helps the gay people nor the LGBTQAI+ community in general. We need to legalize same-sex marriage so as to push ahead towards enjoying fully and completely our human rights.

CHAPTER THIRTY-SEVEN

ANTICIPATORY BAIL

Author: Ritu Bhardwaj, B.A.,LL.B from Guru Gobind Singh Indraprastha University.

Co-author: Rajat Gaur, B.A.,LL.B from Guru Gobind Singh Indraprastha University.

<u>INTRODUCTION</u>

Anticipatory bail is called as pre arrest bail. Ordinary rule is that when a person gets arrested then only he applies for bail. But there are certain circumstances where a person applies for bail before the arrest is made. Application for anticipatory bail is made on mere apprehension of arrest. In such a case the person who is anticipating his arrest is released before arrest is made. Section 438 of Code of Criminal Procedure, 1973 deals provides the law on this issue. As it is said that prevention is better than cure likewise is the job of anticipatory bail. So, the Purpose of section 438 basically is to save a person, his reputation who is falsely implicated in a case.

<u>LAW IN INDIA</u>

As per section 438 of Code of Criminal Procedure, 1973 only session courts and high court has the power to grant the anticipatory bail. If any person has reason to believe that he might get arrested sooner or later for non- bailable offence then he can approach the court. It is the discretion of the court whether to release him or not.

If court is of opinion that on the prior release of such person there is no harm to society and to the case then it will grant the anticipatory bail. But if court believes that the accused may absond, temper the evidences of the case, influence the witnesses or may not cooperate in investigation process then it can deny the anticipatory bail. The court for this examines the gravity of the offence and the role of the applicant in the case. The court will even consider any material criminal involvement on the part of the accused.

The burden of prove will be on accused to prove that appears to be prima facie case against him in the matter. This necessarily does not mean that accused admits that he has committed the offence. Pre arrest protection via anticipatory bail to the accused is not granted for in any case that comes up in future. The accused has to clearly state in the application about specific case in which he seeks protection.

Even if the anticipatory bail has been granted the police officer's power to investigate will not get affected. The accused is expected to cooperate with investigating officer.

TIME RESTRICTION IN REGARD TO ANTICIPATORY BAIL

In Gurbaksh Singh Sibbia case, first time a constitutional bench laid down the scope of section 438. The Supreme Court held that "section 438(1) should be interpreted in the light of article 21of the constitution that is protection of life and personal liberty and said that the court has absolute discretion to direct the duration of the time on the grant of anticipatory bail". The court conclusively said the anticipatory bail should not be limited by time.

The Hon'ble Supreme court in the Sushila Aggarwal case, categorically held that the anticipatory bail need not to be for certain period rather it can be for unlimited period even until the trial.

So, once an anticipatory bail is granted it is for unlimited period unless it is cancelled by that court on the violations of some bail conditions or on expiration of court specified time period. Any superior court can also set aside the anticipatory bail order. Moreover the police can also move to the court for cancellation of anticipatory bail under section 439(2).

AFFECT OF REJECTION OF ANTICIPATORY BAIL APPLICATION

Unexpectedly the police is seen to be overly active in arresting accused when anticipatory application gets rejected. If police arrest the accused once the court has rejected the application, such arrest will be said to be legal. But rejection of the anticipatory bail does not imply mandatory arrest thereafter. Nor does it imply that accused is guilty in that case. Even though the police was not playing active role earlier in investigating the case, sudden worrying of the police and prosecution on the pre arrest release of accused is quite shocking. It usually arrest the applicant on rejection of application by court. It is never seen in the court of law that police agreed with pre arrest bail of accused. That's why the preference of lawyer in a case of anticipatory bail can be called as double edge sword.

CONCLUSION

Anticipatory bail is a immunity from the custody. The application for anticipatory bail is filed on tangible ground of apprehension. Mere anticipation of arrest will form no ground. The anticipatory bail application and even the bail order can get cancelled by the court anytime. The police officers are at liberty to arrest the accused when application is rejected though it does not have the obligatory implication.

Authors' Biography

Ritu Bhardwaj, she has over 2 years of practice at Supreme court, Delhi High Court and Central Administrative tribunal. She mainly has criminal, administrative and writ based work. She completed her Law from Guru Gobind Singh Indraprastha University, New delhi. She bagged many awards of best speaker, debater and in moot court competitions during her law school. At very young age, she has the ability to present a case favourable to hon'ble judges by the use of simple parable and explanation. Apart from a keen writer, she is a human rights activist.

Rajat Gaur, he has over 2.5 years of practice at Supreme Court, Delhi High court, National company Law Tribunal and National Green Tribunal. He mainly deals in criminal, matrimonial and company law. He is a director of LAACA Foundation (operates against child violence, exploitation and harassment). He completed his Law from Guru Gobind Singh Indraprastha University, New delhi. He has attained remarkable success at this age because of the hardwork and values that was developed during his law School.